T0274003

STRONGER TOGETHER

**Building World-Changing
Business Collaborations**

STRONGER TOGETHER

Building World-Changing Business Collaborations

Nicole Mahoney

BookPress®

www.BookpressPublishing.com

Published in Des Moines, Iowa, by:

Bookpress Publishing
P.O. Box 71532, Des Moines, IA 50325
www.BookpressPublishing.com

Publisher's Cataloging-in-Publication Data

Names: Mahoney, Nicole W., author.
Title: Stronger together : building world-changing collaborations that succeed / Nicole W. Mahoney.
Description: Des Moines, IA: Bookpress Publishing, 2023.
Identifiers: LCCN: 2022920224 | ISBN: 978-1-947305-59-5
Subjects: LCSH Business. | Success in business. | Strategic alliances (Business). | Business networks. | Interorganizational relations. | Cooperation. | Competition. | BISAC BUSINESS & ECONOMICS / Organizational Development
Classification: LCC HD69.S8 .M34 2023 | DDC 338.8--dc23

First Edition
Printed in the United States of America
10 9 8 7 6 5 4 3 2 1

For my grandson, Archer.

May stronger collaborations lead to a better world for you.

CONTENTS

CHAPTER 1

Collaboration Builds Communities

Having worked in the travel, tourism, and hospitality industry for thirty years, I have seen first-hand what happens when collaboration is successful. When we reach outside our own silos and seek new ways to work together, collaboration can be powerful.

Big ideas, big projects, and accomplishing something big historically have never been accomplished by one person, one company, or one government alone. Creating something bigger than yourself requires a team working together to achieve a common goal. I learned about the power of collaboration at age twenty-three.

After eight years working in my family business, I decided to take a job with the company that was hired to oversee construction and operations of a new AAA baseball stadium being built in downtown Rochester, New York. It was 1994, the Rochester Red Wings had been playing baseball at Silver Stadium outside of the city center since 1929, and it was time for an upgrade. My hometown was looking to revive the downtown area, and a new baseball stadium promised to attract people from the suburbs and give workers a reason to remain in the city after closing time. My first assignment was organizing the groundbreaking scheduled for November 16. The naming rights sponsor was to be announced, our local telephone company had just rebranded from Rochester Tele-phone to Frontier Communications, and the new name of the stadium—Frontier Field—was revealed at the press event.

The construction of the stadium moved along smoothly, though it wasn't open by the spring of 1996 and the start of that year's baseball season as was originally hoped. It was ready to open by July, but the team opted not to move mid-season, so it was decided to open without them. A second tenant for the facility, the Rochester Rhinos major league soccer team, was the first to play in the stadium, and we hosted a grand opening celebration and the Drum Corps Nationals event that same season.

It was this project that gave me my first insight into the power of working together to create something big. I was part of a community of collaborators including economic devel-opment officials, the tourism office, county government, and private business. We were focused on elevating the experience people would have in downtown Rochester and at the baseball stadium. Building a $35 million dollar sporting facility is one thing, but bringing a community together to make it happen is something totally different, and that is what set the groundwork for what would become a decades-long passion of mine.

The ideas I will share throughout this book come from guests I have interviewed on my podcast *Destination on the Left*. They come from clients my agency and I have worked with since 2009. They come from research we collaboratively produced with partner Susan Baier at Audience Audit where we surveyed 161 travel, tourism and hospitality professionals. The ideas shared in this book come from my own life experiences and those of others who have shared the journey with me.

The type of collaborations this book focuses on are inter-organizational, meaning those between different organizations or businesses. This is not about internal teams collaborating or breaking down barriers between departments or divisions within the same organization. This is about harnessing the power of collaboration when dealing with other organizations—even with your competitors.

The people who recognize and understand the positive impacts that inter-organizational collaborations can make on business success are the ones putting the tools to use most effectively. Collaboration is the exponential multiplier that makes $1 + 1$ greater than 2. It is about accomplishing something bigger together than one can do on their own.

For quite a while, I have been in pursuit of understanding

what makes some collaborations successful while others struggle to get off the ground. The study I published on collaboration in the travel, tourism, and hospitality industry in January 2021 provided the data to help solidify the thinking and ideas I've gathered over the course of my career.

Opportunities Out of Obstacles:
How Data Drove Our Thinking

Research partner Susan Baier and I conducted a survey of 161 travel, tourism, and hospitality professionals to learn more about their perspectives on collaboration. Our research showed that 99 percent of respondents said their organizations had collaborated with others in the industry, while 45 percent said their organizations had extensive experience with collaboration, as well.

We have long touted the power of collaboration in the industry, but our research revealed that inter-organizational collaboration in travel, tourism, and hospitality is more prevalent than we'd thought. However, despite its popularity, there are a number of mixed opinions about the risks and rewards of the practice.

Different Attitudes, Different Segments

We found three distinct attitudes about collaboration, and those attitudes impacted which organizations' collaborations were successful, and which were not.

Curious what sort of collaborator you are?

Visit our online quiz at: https://nicolemahoney.com/
stronger-together-resources

The first group, which we called "the Promoters," was relentlessly enthusiastic about the benefits of collaboration between organizations, while the second group, "the Doubters," was more reserved. The Doubters believed that collaboration was difficult and ineffective, scorning over-zealous organizations for their unrealistic expectations.

A third group, "the Protectors," held collaboration in high regard, but with some restrictions. They believed their organizations' proprietary expertise, systems, and processes represented a competitive advantage and that the exposure of inter-organizational collaborations could therefore put them at risk.

Each of these groups represents about one-third of the industry professionals we surveyed, meaning beliefs are evenly split and collaborative organizations are likely to encounter attitudes different from theirs. Other factors like age, experience, niche, or revenue seem to have little impact on which group a person falls into.

The most fascinating thing, however, is that collaborations are likely to result in success regardless of which groups work together. That means collaborations work even for those who doubt that they do.

While you still need to make sure your organization has good reasons to collaborate, you can feel confident that many professionals are finding new opportunities by collaborating with those around them. Especially in times of trouble, instead of crumbling in the face of adversity, collaborative businesses continue to forge new relationships, service lines, and products that enable them to grow.

Obstacles to Collaboration

When different types of professionals and organizations try to optimize for inter-organizational collaboration, a lot can go wrong. Our study asked what the greatest challenges were for collaboration and why.

First off, there is a lack of faith in our abilities to collaborate well. While 48 percent of the Promoters "completely agree" that they have strong collaborative skills, only 21 percent of Doubters and 21 percent of Protectors share the same sentiment. Note: That is an excuse, not a good reason not to collaborate.

Second, 61 percent of respondents said a lack of funding or other resources was a significant challenge for their organization. Note: Many creative collaborations do not require significant funding.

Third, 57 percent cited poor communication between organizations. Note: You can mitigate this by properly setting expectations at the beginning.

Sizeable groups also cited the other challenges they encountered while working with collaborative teams:

• 45 percent cited the lack of priority compared to initiatives specific to one participating organization or another.

- 41 percent cited a lack of leadership support.

- 40 percent cited a lack of trust between organizations.

- 39 percent cited external forces such as economic or industry developments driving other priorities.

- 35 percent cited the lack of a strong, designated leader for the collaborative effort.

- 33 percent cited different comfort levels with technology.

In nearly all cases, the percentage of each segment citing a particular challenge was eerily similar—everybody seems to be struggling with the same things no matter which segment they were a part of.

We grouped these challenges into the 3-C framework for collaboration—Communication, Commonality, and Commitment—which I developed through my study of collaboration. And while some may encounter specific challenges more often than others, it is clear from our research that overcoming challenges in all three areas is critical for collaborations to be successful.

First, communication is essential to maintain clarity with partners and prospects, and it is an opportunity to be a calming voice amid the uncertainty and chaos.

Next, commonality is about identifying common goals and operating with the greater good at heart.

And finally, commitment means sticking with collaborative efforts no matter how tough the going gets because when we bounce back, we bounce back together.

Professionals and organizations able to check these boxes can thrive under any circumstances, and this framework is the key to identifying opportunity in the face of adversity.

Opportunities to Seize

Members of all three segments "agree completely" that their organizations would benefit from collaborating with the right counterparts—90 percent of Promoters, 50 percent of Doubters, and 45 percent of Protectors, to be specific—and nearly all others "agree strongly."

Flat out, the industry believes we should encourage collaboration rather than dampen it. As one Promoter states, "Everyone is experiencing their own emotions with COVID and our businesses. Now is the time to open up some of the personal chapters of your life and become closer in your partnerships."

A Doubter offers words of encouragement. "Do not be your own stumbling block when it comes to collaboration," they advised. "If you feel like your role or organization will take a back seat moving forward in a group, then you were most likely riding in the back already."

And from a Protector, we received perhaps the most encouraging note for organizations who might be playing outside their league but also considering collaboration with others. The Protector wrote, "This is a time of great opportunity. In particular, those new to the industry will have their ideas listened to in ways they would not have even a year ago."

Africa's Eden Seizes Opportunity During COVID-19 Pandemic

A great example of how collaboration can help overcome obstacles is the story of Africa's Eden, 520,000 square kilometers of Eden-like beauty in the Kaza region. The economy of this region relies heavily on the tourism industry with visitors supporting 2 million people. Without tourism, private businesses and the important work they do both suffer. In addition to being a key economic driver, tourism also sustains efforts to conserve and preserve natural resources in the area. Any disruption in the attraction of visitors can be detrimental to the health of the region.

Late in 2019, news organizations around the world started reporting on the impact of climate change on the Kaza region, and Victoria Falls, one of the seven wonders of the world and the area's main attraction, became the poster child for the result of a dryer climate. *BBC News* released a story titled "Could Victoria Falls dry up?" on November 25, *The Guardian* wrote on December 9, "Victoria Falls dries to a trickle after worst drought in a century," and then *Lonely Planet* again asked the question December 12, "Is Victoria Falls drying up?"

One of the region's tour providers in Zambezi posted a blog on their website in response to this news coverage. The blog announced, "A number of you have expressed concerns...so to clarify...Victoria Falls hasn't dried up! The water levels at the Falls are at their lowest during October, November, and early December—every year. We're just approaching the rainy season, so this is not in any way unusual."

These headlines about the drying of the Falls were having a negative impact on future bookings, and the Kaza region destinations knew they needed to do something world-changing.

In February 2020, the Africa's Eden Regional Tourism Association was established. This was the first collaboration between competing tourism providers across four countries, designed to promote visitation recognizing that all of them shared a common vision for the Kaza region. When the association began, the region was already experiencing declining occupancies and growth due to negative publicity, but then COVID-19 hit.

The organization's new CEO, Jillian Blackbeard, started her job one month before COVID-19 brought a shutdown of almost all tourism operations in the region. Without access to employment within the tourism industry, the region needed to think big to survive. More than ever before, the travel and tourism industry required a unified voice. Sadly, the region has had their fair share of challenges over the years, from economic sanctions to wildlife crime. Yet nothing they had faced was quite like COVID-19. From the land to the wildlife to the people who call the region their home, all were affected.

At the time, the collapse of tourism not only threatened the loss of jobs, but also risked the very existence of the largest protected wildlife estate on the planet. In fact, they had already begun to see an increase in poaching due to

COVID-19, and they needed healing and hope.

The shared vision Blackbeard and her organization painted was a big one. It had never been done before, and it would require resources of which Africa's Eden Regional Tourism Association had very little. If successful, the collaboration would bring together competing marketing and communications providers and platforms to create a pro bono "digital destination" for a diverse association of competing private companies. The project would set out to build a digital version of the region that would mirror the physical one.

Through communication strategies, Blackbeard was able to get a group of global professionals to join this shared vision and to identify roles and clearly delineate expectations, and everyone involved in the project came to the table in a genuine way for the greater good. Africa's Eden Regional Tourism Association and a global team of communication companies worked together to support this beautiful region. Their new digital platform helped Africa's Eden with the resources, marketing content, training, and network needed to move forward—a position they did not have before—and it helped them build relationships, increase awareness, and stay competitive during the COVID-19 shutdown—something they could not have accomplished on their own.

Africa's Eden embraced world-changing collaboration by bringing together four countries that share a common geography and set of challenges and needs. If four countries collaborating was not enough, Blackbeard was also able to build a second collaboration for Africa's Eden through the digital destination project itself. The digital providers shared a common industry expertise in travel and tourism, as well as a passion for innovative solutions to the problems caused by the pandemic. When building a strong collaboration, you want to seek out and commit to relationships that will lead to long-term partnerships. In the Africa's Eden example, Blackbeard was building her consortium with the long-term in mind.

If Africa's Eden can do it, you can too! Get out there and start talking to other organizations in your industry. Most of them are ready to have the conversation, and most agree there is opportunity in collaboration. The following pages in this book offer a framework, practical tools, and creative ideas to build your own successful collaborations.

Listen to my interview with Jillian Blackbeard at: https://nicolemahoney.com/stronger-together-resources

CHAPTER 2

The Three Types of Collaborators

In 2021, I commissioned the independent research firm Audience Audit to conduct research into the state of collaboration in the travel, tourism, and hospitality industry. The goal was to assess attitudes about, and experiences with, collaboration. The data revealed three distinct segments among the survey respondents by analyzing levels of agreement or disagreement with thirty-seven attitudinal statements. Through our study, we identified three types of collaborators—Promoters, Doubters, and Protectors.

Each of these defining attitude segments made up about

one-third of the study respondents indicating that these collaborator types are likely to be found on most collaborative teams. Let's take a look at each of the attitudes, their strengths, and their weaknesses.

PROMOTERS

Promoters are the strongest proponents of inter-organizational collaboration. They believe collaboration introduces new ideas and fresh thinking, that it leverages each organization's particular strengths, and that it allows them to achieve goals they couldn't achieve on their own. They also say that being able to collaborate with others successfully is a sign of a well-run company.

Promoters say they have plenty of experience with collaboration and possess strong leadership and collaboration skills. They believe organizations gain more from collaboration than they invest in time, energy, or resources and that successful inter-organizational collaboration also improves the culture of collaboration within a company. They would much rather work in an organization that collaborates with others than one that does not.

If you're pitching a collaboration to a Promoter, you're in the best position you could be. They will enthusiastically support the initiative and are likely to bring a helpful depth of experience to the effort. Allowing Promoters to take a leadership role within a collaboration will likely be a win-win. They'll appreciate the recognition of their leadership skills and expertise, and the collaboration will benefit from their skills, enthusiasm, and experience.

DOUBTERS

While Doubters often engage in collaborative efforts in their organizations, they are more reserved than others about the potential benefits and more concerned about risks. Doubters are more likely to say that collaboration between organizations is harder than it seems, and that most organizations have unrealistic expectations about how quickly collaborations will deliver benefits. They are more likely to feel that collaborations often benefit one organization more than another and may leave a collaboration feeling taken advantage of. They are more likely to believe that organizations may solely be interested in stealing ideas or processes and worry that their organization might be taken advantage of in such a situation. In particular, Doubters are the most likely of all segments to say it's dangerous for organizations to collaborate with potential competitors.

Since Doubters do engage in collaboration, it is likely you'll encounter a few in your collaborative efforts. It's important to show them that you recognize their concerns and fears about being taken advantage of. Incorporating specific measures to ensure that all parties are transparent about their expectations and abilities, to gain mutual understanding and agreement about the collaboration's goals, and to ensure that work is fairly distributed will be a benefit to all participants.

A Doubter's skepticism about keeping expectations and timelines realistic can be helpful perspectives to counter the relentless optimism you'll see from Promoters.

PROTECTORS

Protectors are enthusiastic about collaboration but say their organizations have proprietary expertise, systems, or processes that represent a distinct competitive advantage. Protectors are diligent about protecting their proprietary approaches from other organizations and have methods they'd never reveal to anyone else.

While Protectors are pro-collaboration, they will undoubtedly have concerns about protecting their proprietary information and approaches. Understanding this and bringing these considerations to the forefront when discussing a collaboration with a Protector will increase the level of trust in your efforts.

Promoter Profile: Kelly Rapone

As Tourism Marketing Director at the Genesee County Chamber of Commerce in the Buffalo Niagara region of New York State, Kelly Rapone embodies the attitudes of the Promoter collaborator type.

She has been part of the Chamber's Tourism program since 1999, and during her tenure, she has mastered collaboration at the local, regional, and state levels. In true Promoter fashion, Rapone is always looking for ways to make her marketing dollars go further, and she has found it in the myriad of collaborative programs she is involved in. Her rural county is located between two well-known cities, Rochester and Buffalo, and the internationally known tourist attraction, Niagara Falls. She must be creative with her marketing campaigns to help her rural county stand out. The key to stretching her budget and reaching new visitors is finding and developing niche markets and encouraging other destinations to invest with her in marketing to that niche.

One of Rapone's most successful collaborative programs is the Haunted History Trail of New York State. When the niche trail first launched in 2013, it was intended to help many historic sites and lesser-known attractions get recognized. Twelve counties initially signed up in the first year with the launch of an inexpensive website and rack card. Since then, the collaborative program has grown to thirty-three counties and more than sixty attractions. The Haunted History Trail features attractions from almost every region of New York including haunted dining, tours, attractions, events, and accommodations, with many of the attractions tying back to New York's local history. By 2015, the Haunted History Trail of NYS had earned an Excellence in Tourism Marketing Award from the New York State Tourism Industry Association. With the help of the state tourism office and a few grants, Rapone was able to expand the niche program's reach. An economic impact study conducted in 2016 found that the direct economic impact from the Haunted History Trail was more than $1.5 million with many visitors returning to the sites along the trail. It is the only state-wide paranormal tourism trail in the country.

That type of ROI and reach fuel Rapone's passion for

collaboration, and she did not stop at one program. Promoters believe collaboration allows them to achieve goals they couldn't achieve on their own, and they believe they gain more in return than the resources they invest.

As a Promoter, Rapone champions collaborations within her own county lines too. Looking for another niche to help expand visitation into the county, she identified golf as an innovative way to reach new markets. She reached out to the high-end golf courses and hotels within her county and started packaging and marketing them to the Canadian leisure market. In 2016, the golf getaway packages program launched, with the tourism office providing booking services for golf trips like tee times and hotel stays. Through the golf program, the Genesee County Office of Tourism estimates that in 2018 the community saw a total economic impact of $256,548, representing an ROI of $53 for every $1 spent.

A Guide to Becoming a Better Collaborator

You may already see yourself or others you have worked with in these descriptions of each type of collaborator. The following section will help you understand which type you are, potential hurdles to watch out for, and how to work with other collaborative styles.

PROMOTERS

Let's go! Collaboration brings great benefits. I can't think of a reason not to pursue collaboration with other organizations, even direct competitors. It provides fresh thinking and new ideas, leverages the strengths of each participating organization, and allows us to achieve things we couldn't on our own. This is something we know how to do well, and I'd rather work in an organization that collaborates than one that doesn't. That's the attitude of the Promoter.

Strengths of the Promoter Mindset

- You have the ability to encourage and motivate other organizations in a collaboration.

- You are mindful of your interactions and lean on the strength of your enthusiasm.

Weaknesses of the Promoter Mindset and How to Overcome Them

- Be mindful of how your level of enthusiasm may make you overly trusting and get in the way of your objective evaluation of a collaboration.

- Recognize when you become frustrated by others who don't share the same enthusiastic viewpoint. Take a breath, step back, and learn from their perspective.

- Think through possible challenges and pitfalls before jumping in with both feet.

- Remember that your natural ability to take on collaborations may lead you to take on too many at once.

- As a Promoter, you often will step up to lead a collaboration. Seek ways to delegate and share the workload to keep everyone in the collaboration engaged.

- Recognize when you have put unrealistic expectations on others. Your enthusiasm may make others feel rushed or undervalued.

What Promoters Should Remember About Others

- Not everyone has the same level of experience or understanding with collaboration. They may have less experience with this type of work and may not know how to apply the tools needed to make the collaborative effort efficient and productive.

- Some people may be more or less gung-ho about collaboration than others depending on the type of collaborator they are.

- You may experience impatience with those who aren't keeping up. When this happens, take a step back and try to understand where the other collaborators are coming from.

- Your enthusiasm drives you to be vocal about your ideas. Remember to stop and listen to other ideas and viewpoints. The best ideas may come from the whispers in the background.

Strategies for Working with a Promoter

- Trust that Promotors are experienced with collaboration and will be good partners.

- Be honest about any reservations you have and talk through your concerns up front.

- Openly share your thoughts and ideas. Promotors value new ideas and fresh thinking.

- View the opportunity to work with a Promoter as a learning and growing experience.

- Recognize that the results from working together will be greater than the sum of your individual efforts.

DOUBTERS

Tread carefully. Collaboration isn't always everything it's cracked up to be. If you're not careful, collaboration can allow one organization to take advantage of another. Expectations can be unrealistic and timelines too optimistic. We're happy to collaborate, but the situation has to be right and everyone has to share the work fairly. That's how a Doubter thinks.

Strengths of the Doubter Mindset

- Your ability for critical thinking is an advantage. Your doubts are opportunities to strengthen the collaboration.

- You desire clear and defined goals. They are the glue.

Weaknesses of the Doubter Mindset and How to Overcome Them

- Verify you are not pre-judging an opportunity before fully considering all aspects.

- Beware of misconceptions you have based on past experience. Not every collaboration is the same.

- Consider the lessons learned from past collaborations and how you can turn those into opportunities for future success.

- Beware of self-imposed failure. Expectations often define success. You will get as much out of the collaboration as you put into it.

- Recognize the possibility that there may be partners outside your industry who bring a fresh perspective.

- Be careful not to hold up the timeline by putting up roadblocks.

- A lack of experience or avoiding being outside your comfort zone could stop you from getting involved in something new.

- When setting up a collaboration, seek to ensure it is fair to all partners and understand that may not mean it has to be equal.

- Recognize when you may be holding back due to fear of being taken advantage of.

- Transparency is the key to successful collaboration.

What Doubters Should Remember About Others

- They wouldn't be here if they didn't believe in it.

- Others see the bigger picture too and are working toward that vision.

- Understand and appreciate the perspectives of everyone in the collaboration.

- Others trust and respect you enough to be in the collaboration.

- You can learn from others' expertise and previous experiences.

- Others may have resources you don't, and it is okay to tap into that.

Strategies for Working with a Doubter

- Ask them to share their concerns about possible challenges or pitfalls up front.

- Step into the Doubter's shoes and work to understand their perspective.

- Appreciate the balance in perspective they bring to the table.

- Demonstrate the value of collaboration with real examples of past collaborations.

- Clearly identify roles and goals at the start of the collaboration.

- Have regular checkpoints throughout to work through any new concerns.

- Be prepared for Doubters to challenge your ideas, and use those moments as opportunities for the group to consider all possibilities.

PROTECTORS

As long as we protect our competitive advantage, collaboration can work. My organization has proprietary expertise and processes that we'd never share with anyone else, even in a collaboration. Our approach is part of our competitive advantage, and we'd never compromise that. As long as we're protected, collaboration is something I'm happy to consider. This is what a Protector believes.

Strengths of the Protector Mindset

- You have the ability to help others set clear expectations up front to avoid confusion.

- You recognize your positioning and expertise and want to step up as a leader.

Weaknesses of the Protector Mindset and How to Overcome Them

- Recognize when you are holding back information and observe how that may be affecting the collaboration.

- Establish boundaries up front and identify what you are and are not willing to share with your collaborative partners.

- Respect others who are willing to be more of an "open book" and embrace the mutual learning that can be realized.

- Consider how setting limitations may inhibit the potential of the collaboration. Remain open to sharing when you become comfortable.

What Protectors Should Remember About Others

- Everyone in the collaboration brings value, unique ideas, and fresh approaches.

- Collaborative partners are usually in it for the greater good, not to steal your secret sauce.

- Your partners can help you grow and improve.

- Recognize that the results from working together will be greater than the sum of your individual efforts.

Strategies for Working with a Protector

- Set clear roles and boundaries up front.

- Focus on building trust by being transparent about your views on the collaboration.

- Share openly and lead by example.

- Respect the Protector's secret sauce and understand their desire to keep that private.

- Have a conversation in the beginning about what is off limits and what is on the table for the collaboration.

- Reciprocate. If the Protector shares something, make sure you share back.

- Be clear on the results everyone in the collaboration can expect.

- Consider the role the Protector is playing in the collaboration. With more buy-in, they may be less protective. For example, if a Protector is leading the effort, there will be more motivation to make it a success, and they will be more likely to share openly.

Best Practices for Successful Collaborations

Regardless of the type of collaborator you are working with, these best practices will help you create a strong and successful collaboration.

- Have a conversation in the beginning to discuss:

    - What is off limits and what is on the table for the collaboration.

    - Concerns about possible challenges or pitfalls.

    - Any reservations held within the group.

    - The results everyone in the collaboration can expect.

    - Roles and goals of the collaboration.

- Throughout the process:

    - Have regular checkpoints to share updates and work through any new concerns.

    - Lead by example.

    - Openly share your thoughts and ideas.

    - Recognize that the results from working together will be greater than the sum of your individual efforts.

    - Remember that you get out what you put in.

CHAPTER 3

Co-opetition and the Business Case for Collaboration

In our 2021 Rising Tide study, we revealed three different attitudinal segments among travel, tourism, and hospitality professionals—three groups that feel very differently about the benefits and challenges of collaboration with other industry organizations.

Promoters are enthusiastic supporters of organizational collaboration, and they pursue it actively and with a range of organization types. Doubters are collaborators with a more measured view of the challenges and opportunities, and they expect results to take longer. Protectors collaborate but feel they have a substantial risk of losing competitive advantage by revealing proprietary expertise and processes.

Regardless of these differences, 99 percent of respondents in our study said their organizations had collaborated with others in the industry.

The research confirmed that collaboration leads to many opportunities, identified the kinds of challenges that can get in the way, and proved that it's critical for organizations to initiate collaborative efforts if they haven't already. In addition, the research provided some clear direction on how to begin.

I am a huge believer in "co-opetition"—where perceived competitors cooperate to create something bigger together than they could have done on their own. This type of collaboration makes the biggest impact, and the guests on my podcast, *Destination on the Left*, believe it too. They have shared countless stories of successful collaborations and best practices for what made them successful.

While it might seem intuitive that collaborators are avoiding working with organizations who provide similar products and services to the same audience, we were surprised to see that the opposite is true. Seventy-six percent of survey respondents said their organization collaborated with direct competitors, while 52 percent collaborated with organizations offering different products or services.

The number of organizations that respondents have collaborated with may be a factor in the prevalence of direct-competitor collaborations. Those who have collaborated with more than five organizations are far more likely to have collaborated with direct competitors (73 percent) compared to those who haven't (29 percent). Perhaps a larger number of former collaborations simply increases the likelihood that organizations will collaborate with a direct competitor sooner or later, but the gap is striking.

Experience may also play a role here. Respondents with the most collaboration experience are most likely to embrace collaboration with direct competitors. Eighty-four percent of those who said they had extensive experience have also collaborated with direct competitors, compared to only 57 percent of those who said they didn't have much experience. And regardless of their attitudes about collaboration, those with more than 30 years of experience in the travel, tourism, and hospitality industry are more likely than those with less than 10 years of experience to collaborate with direct competitors regardless of the age of the respondent.

If you aren't collaborating with competitors, you may be missing out on tremendous opportunities that others are already tuned into.

Respondents whose organizations have collaborated with direct competitors were more likely to say they gained every one of the benefits we explored in our survey, namely:

- increased innovation

- improved relevance to customers

- economic gains

- improved brand identity

- increased levels of trust in the organization by stakeholders, customers, and partners

So you can hear it straight from them, here is what some individuals said:

- "Collaborate with others in your industry, even if they are competitors. You are all working for common goals, and fresh ideas help everyone involved."

- "If you collaborate with a competitor who handles something better than you, you don't have as much research and work to do. You can make more money and develop a better relationship with the competitor who may come to you next time with something they don't normally do."

- "Most people confuse their partners with their competitors, and a bigger pie makes one's own slice larger."

Those statements are backed up by research. Those who have collaborated with direct competitors are more likely to rate their collaborations as extremely valuable, both for their organizations and for their own work and expertise. These respondents are also the most likely to say that collaboration can help organizations survive current challenges and be more successful in the future.

The commonality between all of these organizations is that they have embraced a potential obstacle (revealing something that a competitor could take advantage of) and treated it as an opportunity. This is a thread that runs through our research—we are remarkably resilient, and in the face of difficult times, we have turned to those we might have otherwise considered a threat.

The History of Travel Collaboration

The art of collaboration is not new. In fact, you could say the tourism industry is built on one from the mid-nineteenth century. One summer afternoon, a man named Thomas Cook had an idea to use the power of the railway to help further the cause of his local temperance society. The group's next meeting was taking place twelve miles from where they lived, and Cook offered to charter a train to take the entire group to the meeting, and he included lunch.

The members of the society loved the idea. It would make their lives easier because they didn't have to figure out travel on their own. Cook negotiated a deal with Midland Counties Railway. Each passenger in the group would be charged a fixed rate for the roundtrip rail ticket plus the meal, and Cook would receive a commission on each package sold.

The concept was simple. A collaboration between the railway, Cook, and the local temperance society was born. Everyone was a winner. The railway company was happy to get so many seats filled up in one booking, Cook was happy to receive a share of the profits for arranging the excursion, and the passengers were happy because they didn't have to organize their own journey or worry about lunch. Everything was taken care of in one easy package.

Thomas Cook could not have known it, but the idea that

he had on that summer's day in 1841 planted the seed for what is today the world's fastest growing industry, which sees more than a billion people move across international borders every year and is worth more than a trillion dollars to the global economy—tourism.

Once again, taking a chance on collaboration proved to be a good business decision.

Collaboration's Benefits

Economic gains were identified in the study as one of the benefits of collaboration. Respondents listed many other benefits to successful collaboration beyond economics, including:

- increased levels of innovation or fresh thinking
- improved relevance to customers and prospects
- improved brand identity or organizational reputation
- expanded skills in digital marketing
- increased trust in the organization on the part of stakeholders, customers, or partners
- operational efficiencies and improved listening and communication skills

These benefits can act as a checklist for evaluating future collaborative opportunities. They will also be helpful when you are trying to champion a collaboration to potential partners, your organization's leadership, or other stakeholders.

Putting the collaboration in the frame of the benefits it will bring will likely bring you more success.

Collaborate to Survive and Thrive

Survey respondents shared a widespread belief that collaboration can not only help individual organizations, but also help an entire industry survive and thrive.

Eighty-one percent of Promoters and more than half of respondents in the other segments say that it definitely can.

> "Identifying partnerships is one of the most delicate and important factors right now. 'We are in this together' is something we hear constantly, this is true, but then we must act on it. We need to collaborate, support, and promote each other." —*Promoter*

Even the majority of Doubters believe this to be the case, despite their concerns about collaboration gaining equal work and equal benefits for all parties involved.

> "The only way we all make it through this time is to work together and help each other, promote each other and not be afraid to talk/communicate. We are not alone, but we are in a large sea, and we know there are boats out there… we just need a life jacket or a ladder or helping hand to get into the boat!" —*Doubter*

Collaboration is not only a way to survive in lean times,

but also to address new challenges.

Survey respondents had a number of suggestions for identifying collaboration opportunities.

1. Don't focus too much on balancing the work equally.

Of the factors important for successful collaborations, "All participating organizations doing an equal amount of the work required," was rated least important by all segments. "The collaboration is designed to benefit all participating organizations equally," was also rated much less important than nearly all other factors. These were both viewed as far less important than participants fully agreeing on the goals of the effort and establishing and tracking key milestones.

> "The region we worked in benefited in general from greater awareness and brand identity. Some partners received a bigger share of financial benefit, but all increased their market share." —*Promoter*

2. Find partners who share something in common with you.

Having something in common was rated as very important to successful collaboration, and with 76 percent of respondents collaborating with direct competitors, nearly all were working with organizations playing in the same sandbox. However, respondents were enthusiastic about the belief that even direct competitors have things they do better and are interested in prospects somewhat different from those their own organizations were pursuing.

> "Find similarities with other organizations that customers might look for, but then find a way to highlight these while still keeping your unique value proposition."
> —*Doubter*

> "Find those that fill your service gaps, develop trust, communicate more than necessary and expand accordingly." —*Protector*

3. Communicate, communicate, communicate.

Aspects of communication consistently bubbled up to the top of the list when it came to factors that made collaborations successful, but they also came up often when respondents identified challenges that can get in the way.

Collaborators need to commit to honest and transparent communications, feel comfortable talking with and leaning on one another, and accurately represent their organization's abilities and limits.

> "It doesn't have to be combative, competitive, or scary. If communication is clear and honest and the objectives are clear and shared, it can be very, very impactful and rewarding." —*Promoter*

> "Collaboration and communication are extremely important

in these relationships. Stewarding sponsors and sharing is important. The more communication there is, the more effective we are operationally." —*Doubter*

"Outline specific goals and tasks, stay committed, and constantly communicate." —*Protector*

4. Use tools to make communication easier.

Collaborators are using a range of tools to communicate with team members. Eighty-two percent are using email, but the most successful are far more likely to also be using file-sharing platforms like Dropbox or Google Drive, virtual meeting platforms like Zoom, and even project management and group messaging tools.

"Just do it. Utilize virtual meetings, Zoom meetings, email, and phone communication." —*Promoter*

Ohio Birding Collaborative

When Melinda Huntley worked for the Ottawa County Visitor's Bureau along Lake Erie in Northern Ohio, she started to notice cars with out-of-state license plates parked alongside the road for miles as she drove to work each day. One day, she decided to stop and find out what all of those visitors were doing, and she was handed a pair of binoculars. Huntley discovered that region of Ohio was one of the top birding sites in North America.

Huntley and her team at the tourism office knew there was an opportunity, and they decided to invite the right people to the table to explore the potential of promoting a birding trail along the Lake Erie shores and islands. They invited all the managers from the parks and preserves to a meeting along with neighboring visitors' bureaus to begin a discussion about a collaborative program. That first meeting did not go as smoothly as Huntley had planned; in fact, she described it as a screaming match. What she soon discovered was the people around the table had different perceptions of what tourism meant for their organizations. The tourism office saw the opportunity to bring new customers to the businesses in the region, providing greater economic impact. The park and preserve managers were afraid that a birding program would overwhelm their places with droves of visitors that would tax their natural resources.

Even though the first meeting did not go well, the group did not give up. They continued to keep an open dialogue about the possibilities, and several months later, in the mind of one of the park managers, the idea clicked. He had a zoning issue that was going to threaten the integrity of his park with a proposed development, and he realized that if he could prove the economic value of the park being preserved, he could get buy-in from stakeholders to help protect the area. Suddenly, that park manager became a huge advocate for the program, and the collaboration found its path forward.

Bringing the right people to the table, listening, communicating, and problem-solving together helped the Ohio birding collaborative to take off. Now visitors can find resources on the regional website that highlights sixty-three birding spots within the area and promotes the region as the warbler capital of the world.

As Huntley and her team found out, when you start with communication, your collaborations really can fly.

> Listen to the full story on episode 268 at
> https://nicolemahoney.com/stronger-together-resources

Successful Co-opetition with Multiple Stakeholders

A shining example of a multi-stakeholder collaboration is the Haunted History Trail of New York State, a collection of more than eighty-five individual creepy, spooky, and paranormal hotspots across the state. It is the only statewide paranormal trail in the country, featuring hotels with hauntings, restaurants filled with ghostly activity, museums, historical sites, and even an asylum that all offer a dedicated and authentic haunted experience for visitors. While most people consider haunts to be a fall or October activity, the Haunted History Trail promotes spooky tourism 365 days a year through a website, a trail guide, a public relations campaign, and an active social media presence.

This collaboration drives more demand, visitation, and business to trail partners. According to a 2017 Economic Impact study conducted by Young Strategies, the Haunted History Trail partners reported an increase in year-over-year attendance with two-thirds (64 percent) attributing the increase in attendance to the Haunted History Trail program.

The Haunted History Trail targets an audience of the "paranormal curious"—not professional ghost hunters, but leisure travelers who want to add one or two haunted experiences to their trip or plan a dedicated ghostly getaway. They are based in drive markets in upstate New York, New York City, Pennsylvania, and New England, and fall into a typical age range of 25 to 60. The goal of the Haunted History Trail is to inspire overnight travel among these leisure travelers, drive them to the trail's haunted location partners, promote statewide travel across New York, and create year-round demand for a paranormal product.

Photography is essential to those marketing efforts. It is featured prominently across the Haunted History Trail's website (www.hauntedhistorytrail.com) and in an annual thirty-six--page printed visitor guide detailing haunted stops and visitor experiences. Photos are used on social media including Facebook and Instagram, and in Facebook advertising that encourages brochure downloads and drives ticket sales for haunted events. Perhaps most importantly, the images provide a new way of looking at a location that creates feelings of trepidation and unease that are frequently played up across various communication channels.

The strategy across the trail is to share the fun, casual, and curious side of the paranormal. The 2019 Haunted History Trail guide was requested and mailed out to more than 49,600 potential visitors and guests. The earned media placements for 2019 totaled more than 18 million impressions, and social media saw 10 percent growth across all of its major channels.

As of October 2019, The Haunted History Trail website saw 177,285 total users (a 9 percent increase over 2018) and 223,247 total sessions (a 4 percent increase over 2018) and housed the largest collection of haunted and Halloween events in New York State.

CHAPTER 4

Collaborative Marketing in Tourism

In the travel, tourism, and hospitality industry, it can be difficult to grab the attention, and reservation, of a visitor. With limited time and a set budget, travelers have the tough decision of choosing where to go. Destinations often feel like they are competing against others, when in reality, a rising tide lifts all boats. By working together with other destinations, visitation can increase in a way that impacts all attractions and businesses in the area. Travelers need several things to do, restaurants to visit, and places to sleep during their trip, but they aren't likely to visit the same attraction or restaurant in one trip. Businesses and tourism attractions that work together on collaborative marketing create a better experience for the visitor and encourage multiple overnights, which leads to more revenue for the area as a whole.

Collaborative marketing leverages the resources of multiple partners to create successful marketing programs. I like to think of these programs as another example of co-opetition. Partners cooperate with their perceived competitors to create a product larger than one they can execute on their own. Partners could include neighboring counties, different destinations, or themed attractions.

Benefits of Working Together:

A bigger budget. When partners pool their budgets together, they are able to do bigger and better things that are mutually beneficial. More money could mean a new website, more digital advertising, additional collateral, or attendance at more trade shows.

More exposure. The more partners involved, the more people to promote your product. Each entity can talk about it on their social media channels, post it on their website, include it in their collateral, or mention it during trade and media shows.

Broader appeal. Travelers are more likely to take a trip when there are multiple points of interest. Think about it. The more things there are to do, the more appealing the trip is. Travelers may be more interested in a destination when it's packaged within a region because there are more things to see and do.

Check out these examples of collaborative marketing in tourism:

Trails

Trails string together multiple stops with a specific theme in an easy-to-travel way. They do most of the work for visitors, allowing people to choose their beginning and end points. Trails are also very trendy because they encourage visitation to multiple stops. That means they are more likely to attract visitors who wouldn't necessarily make a one-off stop. Travelers want to feel a sense of accomplishment as they check off trail stops, especially if they receive a prize for completing the route.

Wayne County's Apple Tasting Tour—local farms, farm markets, and wineries that showcase apple products during the month of October—uses a marketing collaboration to drive visitation into the county and to participating businesses.

As the largest apple-producing county in New York State, the trail program relies on participation and buy-in from local businesses. These businesses come together around the common theme of apples. A true testament to the success of this trail promotion is that a majority of businesses have consistently participated in it for more than twenty years. While struggles between perceived competitors could easily arise, the Apple Tasting Tour offers a creative approach to increasing tourism, and the businesses see the value in working together.

For more than twenty years, a printed passport encouraged consumers to visit stops on the trail to collect stamps for a chance to win prizes. In the fall of 2020, amid the COVID-19 pandemic, the trail stops were positioned to offer safe outdoor experiences, but the county recognized the need to replace the physical passport with a virtual option while maintaining the opportunity to win prizes. The target audiences for the trail included adults who enjoy the fall, apples, and agriculture with a specific focus on teachers, parents, and grandparents within a sixty-mile radius of the county. They knew that the added interest in outdoor experiences during the COVID-19 pandemic would offer an added draw for the trail.

Proven marketing strategies and tactics used in past years continued: local public relations outreach, email newsletters, and Facebook and Instagram posting and advertising. New messaging focused on the theme "U Pick the Way," playing off the popular apple-picking activity while showing people they could participate as much as they were comfortable with. A new app was launched to offer a virtual way to experience the trail. It incorporated the look and feel of the Apple Tasting tour brand and included photography, an interactive map, and easy-to-navigate listings to give the user a simple way to access the trail. The experience was enhanced by including nearby parks to give visitors more open-air options. The app also included information on three local restaurant sponsors, the contest, and how to enter.

The new passport app geofenced questions requiring people to be at the location to unlock the trivia. Questions were simple with easy re-tries to keep a low barrier to entry.

Correct answers received a badge for the location, and people submitted screenshots of badges weekly to win prizes.

The 2020 Apple Tasting Tour was another successful collaboration. The app had more than 8,000 unique visitors with 24,000 page views, an average of thirteen minutes on the site, and 9.31 average pages per visit. The map was the third most-visited page, with 3,094 views and an average of three minutes spent on the page, and the contest received 83 entries.

International Product Development

The Wild Center, a natural history museum located in the Adirondacks, led the creation of a program designed to attract international travelers to the north country of New York state. In a remote place like this, organizations don't have millions of dollars through a visitor's bureau as in a bustling destination like New York City. Resources in small towns like those in the Adirondacks are scarce, and businesses have to get creative when reaching new markets.

The Wild Center identified a need to attract international visitors. They knew that reaching this new market could bring more revenue and visitation especially during soft periods when the traditional visitor was conspicuously absent. Hillarie Logan-Dechane, The Wild Center's Deputy Director, knew that her museum and the Adirondack region offered experiences that international visitors from certain markets would really like.

Through a collaboration with the New York State office

of tourism, better known as I Love NY, the Wild Center identified the Chinese market and part of the European market as
strong target audiences. Knowing that these groups fit a
profile that projected they would be attracted to what the
region and neighboring areas had to offer, The Wild Center
began looking for partners who shared a common goal of
attracting international visitors. They applied for grant money
and decided to dedicate some of their own capital for the
creation of Go North, a product that would appeal to the
wholesale travel trade that sells travel products to international markets.

A collaboration was born between the Wild Center, the
northern part of the New York State capital region, Saratoga,
Queensbury, and the Lake George region. Through the
collaboration, a travel itinerary was developed specifically
for the international travel trade, the wholesale market, to
market to their audiences. In this example, The Wild Center
decided to take action instead of accepting that they were not
getting their fair share of the international market. They
received positive feedback from the region and from people
in the international travel trade. It may not be normal for a
museum to spearhead a program like this, but the Wild Center
knew that it needed to happen, and it would benefit many
businesses and communities in northern New York. International travelers were looking for experiences outside of NYC,
and they wanted interesting places to stay, eat, and visit.

Attracting international markets would benefit the
museum by starting a new revenue stream that would arrive
at different times from their traditional audiences. When

reflecting on the beginning of the collaboration, Logan-Dechane said, "It's going to help everybody, and that's the kind of sea change in thinking that we've gone through over the last twenty years or so. This is not a little trite statement, but if we can work together, we'll all succeed."

To learn more about The Wild Center and this collaborative program:

Listen to my interview with Logan-Dechene at https://nicolemahoney.com/stronger-together-resources

Motorcoach Market

When new accommodations and attractions signaled a growth of tourism assets, the Cayuga County Office of Tourism wanted to expand its outreach into an untapped market by reaching out to group tour operators. They knew that a collaborative marketing program targeted toward the motorcoach industry would increase the travel and tourism dollars spent in the area, but it required starting from zero.

Cayuga County sought to build an economic generator that would attract group business for multi-day trips by focusing direct sales activities that supported ongoing collaborative marketing efforts. As a completely new effort, every part of the program—its strategies, metrics, tools, and tactics—needed to be identified and created. So the county identified three goals:

1. Create a group tour program that brings positive economic impact for the county.

2. Build stakeholder awareness of the group tour market and how to work with its operators.

3. Position Cayuga County as a wonderful and welcoming group tour destination.

The strategy focused on building relationships with and among stakeholders and group tour operators while positioning Cayuga County as a welcoming community that took pride in their accommodations and attractions. The area also demonstrated the experiences and leveraged tourism assets that offered tours comparable to those of the well-known Finger Lakes region.

To be successful, the program relied on the participation of businesses throughout the community and welcomed guests who were travelling in groups and mostly arriving on buses. The collaborative marketing program:

- leveraged existing products to showcase group tour opportunities.

- created relationships with tour operators and stakeholders to help build awareness and audience.

- developed itineraries and hosted familiarization tours to support Cayuga County group tour experiences.

- utilized collateral to provide tangible information sources for follow up conversations.

- deployed a lead nurturing tool for continuous communications and product awareness.

- tracked metrics to measure program success.

Over the first eight years of the program, each year saw an increase in bookings and visitor spending. In 2019, the program brought in more than $500,000 in visitor spending with more than 2,000 room nights.

Collateral Development

Travel Alliance Partners (TAP) is a partnership of North American Tour Operators who specialize in specific areas of geographical expertise and work together to develop tour packages of the highest quality and with the best value and biggest variety. Together as TAP, they aim to fill more scheduled departures, reduce cancellations, and expand product portfolios, and they were the first in the industry to offer guaranteed trip departures regardless of seats filled or sold.

TAP is able to make this promise working hand-in-hand with Preferred Professional Travel Providers (PPTPs) as destination and attraction partners. Several of these PPTPs are members of TAP's Guild program, which provides additional opportunities to build stronger relationships with Tour Operator Partners, as well as additional marketing material and special invitation benefits to showcase the assets of their tourism product. Each year, TAP produces *Dream Destinations*, a magazine that features Guild members' preferred destination regions, which have each won high acclaim for the beauty and travel experiences they offer.

Aimed at travelers, *Dream Destinations* is designed to entice North Americans to create memorable experiences using TAP vacations. The brochure is distributed each year to travel buyers through digital and partner channels.

In 2019, *Dream Destinations* was in need of an update. The old template was designed to serve the members over the consumer experience. The new design considered the consumer as the primary driver and mapped out a series of experience-driven categories that the member locations could fit into—craft beverage, outdoor adventure, food, scenery, sports, annual events, arts and culture, accommodations, history, and animal encounters.

Each member was asked to consider which categories they felt were core to their destination and select their top three for inclusion. From there, a layout was created that could be easily understood by and enticing to potential visitors hearing about these locations for the first time. The Table of Contents offered visitors the option to "Browse by Topic" or "Browse by Location," listing page numbers to help them quickly find the content that best fit their interests.

Dream Destinations is a companion piece to TAP's *Guaranteed Departures* brochure and acts as an inspiration guide, leading readers directly to TAP's guild members. In 2019, it was mailed to more than 15,000 travel buyers, American Bus Association operators, and National Tour Association operators across the US and Canada. More than 7,000 copies were distributed directly through tour operators. The magazine appeared at consumer trade shows across North America and was distributed at group leader and travel agency shows. The magazine is also available via the Travel Alliance Partners website in a digital version.

Competing Destinations Collaborate
for Broader Appeal

In March 2020, in the midst of lockdowns and travel restrictions, Kurt Krause, President and CEO of Visit Norfolk, noted it was tough to figure out when his destination marketing organization should resume marketing. But rather than sit idle, his team prepared for the right time. They assessed the strengths of the area and the changing desires of travelers, and Krause recognized the value of its plentiful waterfront and its great history. Visit Norfolk offered outdoor activities and attractions, and there was always demand from Memorial Day to Labor Day for people seeking the beach, water, and the Chesapeake Bay. Krause knew that eventually people would get tired of being locked up in their houses. He also recognized that Norfolk was one gas tank away from 72 million people. The traveler sentiment studies published at the time indicated that 30 to 40 percent of Americans wanted to travel in the coming six months. Krause saw the opportunity that 30 to 40 percent of 72 million people offered.

With this information, an unheard-of idea for a collaborative marketing campaign was born—Norfolk would collaborate with Virginia Beach. These two destinations had a long rivalry as competitors. But this opportunity promised more than enough visitors for both destinations. Each destination contributed $500,000 for a combined million-dollar campaign with more reach than each destination would have on their own.

Virginia Beach offered an Atlantic coast beach resort

experience with lots of things to do. Norfolk offered urban waterfront, arts, culture, restaurants, and history. The two destinations felt that together they were better, so they put a campaign together set to the track of Etta James's song *Together at Last*. The name of the campaign alluded to the notion that finally Virginia Beach and Norfolk were cooperating, but the theme was intended more for families, couples, and friends who would once again feel reunited.

The campaign recognized that people were going to be anxious to get out, get some fresh air, and breathe a sigh of relief. They weren't going to travel internationally, and they weren't going to be comfortable on a plane. Traditionally, people travel south to the beach; rarely do they go north. So the campaign focused on Pittsburgh, Columbus, Philadelphia, and Baltimore.

The *Together at Last* campaign was so successful, the two destinations decided to extend it by a month. The $1 million investment into the campaign generated $6 million in hotel room sales. According to STR, a service that tracks occupancy for markets across the US, the Norfolk Virginia Beach market, one of the top twenty-five markets in the country, led the country as the number one market for twenty consecutive weeks that summer.

To learn more about this campaign:

Listen to my podcast interview with Kurt Krause at
https://nicolemahoney.com/stronger-together-resources

CHAPTER 5

The "3-C" Framework for Collaboration

I have spoken with folks from all parts of the travel and tourism industry and asked them to provide examples of successful collaborations and best practices. I have been on a quest to learn more about what makes some collaborations win while others struggle to find their footing. It started in 2016 with the launch of my podcast *Destination on the Left*, where I interview professionals from all parts of the tourism, travel, and hospitality industry on creativity and collaboration. After seven years and more than 300 episodes, I've begun to see many themes emerge that point to what makes successful collaborations work.

The "3-C Framework for Collaboration" is a crowdsourced solution based on countless podcast interviews, conversations, first-hand experience, and research for creating world-changing collaborations. Through my conversations, I've discovered three key parts to creating and maintaining collaboration: Communication, Commonality, and Commitment.

I wanted to test the framework, so I developed a study along with research partner Audience Audit, which we released in January 2021. I wanted to find out whether the areas I had identified were broadly recognized across the industry. By organizing challenges cited by respondents into these three groups, we saw that respondents had experienced all three, with the greatest frequency in the Commitment and Commonality areas. Communication was cited by 34 percent of study respondents, Commonality by 42 percent, and Commitment by 42 percent.

The illustration on the next page summarizes the framework at a glance.

The First C: **Communication**

On my podcast, I ask each guest the question, "How do you set the groundwork for a successful collaboration?" The number one answer that I receive is communication. There are four strategies that will help you master this part of the framework.

The 3-C Framework for Collaboration

1. Build a plan for communication.

We all intuitively know that communication is paramount to getting our ideas across, building consensus around a vision, and motivating others to help achieve our ideas, yet we don't have a plan for how we will communicate.

Your plan for communication starts with who you're communicating with—your audience. Consider the organizations you're collaborating with, identify the point person for each one, and define their roles up front. Next, establish messages. Are there regular status updates, a shared project plan, or key milestones that need to be communicated?

Part of your communication plan includes the format for sharing information. Is it an email, conference call, or

in-person meeting? Do you have a shared Google Doc that everyone updates regularly? Establish how frequently you will communicate, as well. Is it daily, weekly, monthly, or at key milestones?
    Finally, identify who owns the communication. Is there one leader for the collaboration? Or will you split up the responsibility between a few people on the team?

2. Set realistic expectations establishing roles and goals up front.

Setting realistic expectations and establishing roles and goals up front will set up your world-changing collaboration for success. Be clear on the goals you are aiming for, identify roles for each person, and set expectations. This is where many collaborations stumble, but spending time up front discussing these details will make a big difference as you set out to implement your plan.

3. Have a shared vision.

As a collective, you all must buy into the vision that you are trying to achieve together. Paint the picture of that world-changing idea you are working toward. What will realization of it look like? How will you know when you have achieved it? What are the smaller achievements that you will experience along the way?

4. Transparency is key.

Be genuine and prepared for courageous conversations, and bring your best self to the collective. Hidden agendas will not work here. You must be in it for the collective good, and any thoughts or concerns that you have regarding your role should stated openly at the beginning. To achieve your common goals and reach the world-changing vision you have in front of you, transparency is key.

Finger Lakes Leverages Communication Amid the Pandemic

Destination Marketing Organizations (DMOs) are evolving, redefining their roles as the landscape continues to shift. First, it started with the move to digital marketing and communications—sharing information where and when the traveler was looking for it. Then, for destinations experiencing over-tourism, roles shifted from marketing to managing. Most recently, destinations have focused more on place-making—creating places where people want to live, work, and play.

DMOs shifted again as the COVID-19 pandemic swiftly changed their world. In March 2020, the New York State on PAUSE (Policies that Assure Uniform Safety for Everyone) executive order closed all in-office functions for non-essential businesses, banned all non-essential gatherings of any size, and suspended travel. As an organization whose main purpose is to promote travel and tourism, the Finger Lakes Visitors Connection (FLVC) had to evolve.

The organization's leader, Valerie Knoblauch, first turned to their major funder, Ontario County, to see how her team could assist in the environment that lay before them. They discovered a new collaborative role with the county's economic development department. The best way for them to help was to use their communication skills to address and assist with the massive job loss and closing of businesses in their community.

It was clear that the need extended far beyond traditional hospitality and tourism partners. The need was to address the survival of every small business that created quality of life in the community and that residents and visitors both valued. To bring together all segments of small business, they needed to collaborate with other organizations. In an unprecedented collaboration, FLVC partnered with the Ontario County Economic Development Corporation to support the small business community.

Traditionally, economic development offices look to build up small businesses through financial programs with low-interest loans. FLVC understood that these businesses did not need more debt, they needed to generate revenue by re-opening and getting customers back in the door.

Goals were established to support the small business community in three ways:

1. **Stabilize small businesses** and their employees.
   FLVC stepped in to help interpret and relay the governor's executive orders so businesses understood how to respond to the pandemic.

2. **Streamline re-opening** by reviewing all guidelines, organizing materials, creating templates for businesses to use, and even sharing re-opening strategies including employee wellness programs, visitor safety precautions, and economic stability plans.

3. **Encourage innovation, creativity, and flexibility.** FLVC supported businesses as they worked to reinvent themselves by helping them clearly define who they were and what they offered in the new economy.

The community-wide goal was to have all industries re-open effectively and efficiently. By taking the burden of working through the new protocols off small business owners, they could focus on figuring out the core operations of their businesses.

The collaboration deployed four communication tools designed to support small businesses through the pandemic:

1. **#VisitConfidently brand.** The phrase "Visit Confidently" was important to the community. It spoke to all audiences—businesses, workers, residents, and travelers—to let them know they could feel comfortable within Ontario County, whether they were going to the store, a restaurant, work, or the dentist.

2. **#VisitConfidently Resource Center.** Overnight, cleaning supplies and PPE became coveted items. People were running from store to store to stock up

on the materials they needed to re-open. A "Sanitation Resource Bank" was created where businesses could pick up their necessary PPE, signage, and cleaning supplies. This one-stop-shop made it easy, accessible, and affordable to pick up items that were required to meet new protocols for sanitation, hygiene, and employee safety.

3. **Business owner education.** Re-opening templates, sample forms, and links to other websites were provided in the #VisitConfidently Resource Center to help small businesses navigate the guidelines. Webinars brought together all sectors of the local industry—gyms, bridal shops, salons, you name it— covering travel restrictions, re-opening requirements, inspections, and even HVAC and air filtration options.

4. **Workforce re-education.** Once businesses re-opened, an e-learning training module for workforce re-education on customer service in a COVID-active world was offered complimentary for employees in the county. It was designed to address the challenges of providing the best guest experience in a safe environment while following protocols. In the course, employees learned how to effectively communicate with guests and provide friendly, world-class Finger Lakes service even during challenging times.

Many silver linings were found from working outside of the traditional tourism and hospitality industry and partnering with the economic development office to help small businesses get back on their feet:

1. **New countywide partnerships** helped FLVC continue to create community impact in a post-pandemic world. The pandemic brought the organization together with Chambers of Commerce, Business Improvement Districts, economic development officials, city and town governments, and others.

2. **Awareness of the FLVC increased** through its major role in the community during the pandemic. For the first time, the organization was invited to the table to work with partners different from those they had in the past. This increased awareness lead to stronger programs in the future.

3. **The #VisitConfidently Resource Center** filled a need in the community and revealed the direct and indirect impacts of tourism. It clearly showed the need to extend beyond the traditional hospitality industry. Seeing the sanitation bank's initial worth, the Ontario County Economic Development Corporation awarded a $25,000 grant to expand FLVC's endeavors. Small not-for-profits, a bridal shop, manufacturing and landscaping businesses, and educational organizations had all accessed the

bank—a few immunocompromised residents even used it for their sanitation needs.

4. **Opening up dialogue and creating a community connection** between small businesses had a major impact. Through #VisitConfidently Resources, a variety of businesses across multiple industries were brought together, and though they offered different things, they found commonality in what they needed to re-open.

The Second C: **Commonality**

By definition, commonality is the sharing of features or characteristics two or more parties have in common.

Successful world-changing collaborations find partners who have features, characteristics, or attributes in common with one another. Finding the commonality is the first step. Once you have decided to build a collaboration, next you want to seek and commit to relationships that will lead to long-term partnerships.

A Commonality Partnership Example

When you open yourself up to finding commonality, you may find it in less-obvious places. That's what happened when the Pocono Mountains Visitors Bureau applied commonality to identify partners that could help them realize a vision. They found them outside of the tourism industry, and that resulted in a program with impact well beyond the visitor experience.

There was a big issue with litter on Route 80 heading into Pennsylvania. The corridor is the gateway to the Poconos and the first impression for travelers coming to the region. The Visitors Bureau recognized that local communities, resort owners, and area attractions were already doing a great job keeping up their own curb appeal, but no one was looking at the gateway. So the Visitors Bureau developed the Pickup the Poconos campaign. They built a website, bought billboards, and started doing radio and local TV ads to shine a light on the litter problem.

To help solve it, they put together a Pickup the Poconos day. As they started planning, they realized they needed a vendor who was authorized to work on Route 80 because individuals are not allowed to go on those roads, and the first collaboration for their program was born. They found the Adopt a Highway Corporation that had the contract and authority to pick up litter along the roads. That led the Visitors Bureau to the Penn Department of Transportation, and the campaign kept expanding. They focused on getting more businesses to help in the Adopt a Highway program across all four counties of the Poconos region.

Eventually, the campaign gained momentum across the State of Pennsylvania, and as the visitors bureau looked at ways to improve the reach within their destination, they sought other partners who shared commonality with the initiative and found the local United Way and the local waste authority. Together, they formed the Pocono Mountains

Community Caring Project that focused on removing litter from the Poconos, which now includes a partnership with a homelessness program administered by the United Way. The expanded program hires individuals on the cusp of homelessness to help pick up litter with the county waste authority. The program continues to bring awareness to keeping the Poconos clean while giving back to the community and helping people get back on their feet.

When you find commonality, you never know where it can lead, and when you open yourself up to those world-changing collaborations, you really can move mountains—or at least keep them clean.

To hear more about the Poconos from Brian Bossuyt from the Pocono Mountains Visitors Bureau:

> Listen to my podcast interview with Brian Bossuyt at
> https://nicolemahoney.com/stronger-together-resources

The Third C: **Commitment**

When embarking on a world-changing collaboration, commitment is necessary for success as there will always be roadblocks and obstacles to overcome. There may even be a new pattern emerging that throws a pandemic into the mix every so often in addition to many other uncertainties we will need to navigate. Successful collaborations have team members who feel accountable for their contributions, well-informed leadership that supports the effort, and full commitment by all participants. Dedication to a cause or activity is the definition of commitment; in other words, when you are committed to something, there is no question whether it will succeed or not because your commitment will see you through.

Imagine you have joined a volunteer fire department. You are committed to the cause, and you trust that the other volunteer firefighters are also committed. Imagine running into a burning building, ready to fight a fire. What would happen if you weren't committed to fighting it? What if your fellow firefighters, your partners, your collaborators, also weren't committed? What are the chances you would succeed in getting that fire extinguished? You might think twice about running into that burning building in the first place. Commitment is critical to creating a successful world-changing collaboration.

When joining a collaboration, commit to the hard work it will take to accomplish the shared vision. A great way to make sure everyone is committed is to set deadlines for tasks and milestones. Remain open-minded and ask for solutions when roadblocks appear. We are at our creative best when faced with adversity or a challenge. Successful collaborators don't let those moments go to waste; they stay committed and continue moving forward. Your attitude can make the difference between success and failure. Successful collaborators have a can-do attitude and focus on the long-term vision to help them stay the course.

If you want to learn about hard work, commitment, and adversity, ask a farmer. That's what I did when I talked to Scott Osborn from Fox Run Vineyards on Seneca Lake in the

Finger Lakes wine country. In many areas of the world, wine and wineries are a big part of the tourism product, and the Finger Lakes is no different. I was curious to know how wineries establish world-changing collaborations, so I chose a winery owner who had been in the business for more than thirty years. When Osborn bought his winery, perceptions about New York wines—if there were any perceptions at all—were that they were of low quality and only sweet. Back then, it was hard to convince people from the closest metropolitan market to make the drive to the region to experience the wines made in their own backyard. Osborn called it the invisible hour. In other words, people from Rochester, New York, would not drive more than an hour for a day trip. One day, Osborn drove to Rochester to visit his father and happened to look at the clock as he left the winery. After arriving in Rochester, he looked again and noticed it was a fifty-five-minute trip. A lightbulb went off in Osborn's head, and he started a radio campaign advertising that his winery was only fifty-five minutes from downtown Rochester, inviting people to come down and taste some really outstanding wine.

Osborn's customer counts doubled that year, and he realized the customer wanted more to experience. His staff started recommending the winery two minutes down the road. All of a sudden, people started to realize there was a local wine industry that made for a perfect day trip. Over the years, Osborn has seen his typical winery visitor change from nearby day trips to people from Pennsylvania, New Jersey, New York City, and Europe.

Osborn pointed to many world-changing collaborations that resulted in the Finger Lakes wine region attracting visitors from near and far. One of the more interesting collaborations came about as he was trying to sell his wine in Europe. He'd been attending shows in Europe with the New York Wine and Grape Foundation. After going to one of the shows for three years in a row, he kept hitting roadblocks when trying to get his wines exported to Europe. Distributors were looking to buy the wines, but Osborn needed an importer to sell to the distributors. When he talked to the importers, they would only commit to bringing in three cases to see if it could sell.

It's expensive to send just three cases of wine to Europe from the United States. So Osborn decided to get three of his winery friends together to start a company to export their wine themselves. By doing so, they could reduce the cost of shipping by putting together a group container of wine which allowed Finger Lakes wines to be offered at a lower price point, making it easier for Europeans to buy.

The partners in the export company would frequently visit Europe and facilitate tastings in wine shops. One year after they started, Osborn was back in New York in his own tasting room, and a customer from Belgium came in. The customer said, "We met you at Melanie's Wine Shop and were so impressed with your wines that we decided to take our vacation in the Finger Lakes." Osborn says that happens to him at least four or five times a year now.

Staying committed and being open to new ideas have helped Osborn and Fox Run succeed over 30 years and these world-changing collaborations have made a big difference for the Finger Lakes wine region.

> Listen to my podcast interview with Scott Osborn at https://nicolemahoney.com/stronger-together-resources

When it comes to successful collaborations, all three Cs of the framework were cited as equally important by study respondents. This confirms that the themes we pulled from countless podcast interviews and conversations are foundational to creating a successful collaboration. But when we examined the greatest challenges respondents have experienced with collaboration, we saw something different.

Statistically, Communication was far less likely than the other two Cs to be cited as one of the greatest challenges. This is interesting because the finding suggests that if people tend to believe Communication to be the big sticking point, they're missing two less-considered categories more likely to cause problems. If you spend time focusing on finding commonality and fully committing to the collaboration, you will be setting yourself up for a more successful partnership.

Study Respondents Reinforce Framework

"Collaboration and communication are extremely important in these relationships. Stewarding sponsors and sharing is important. The more communication there is, the more effective we are operationally." —*Protector*

"It doesn't have to be combative, competitive, or scary—if communication is clear and honest and the objectives are clear and shared, it can be very, very impactful and rewarding."—*Promoter*

"Collaborate with others in your industry, even if they are competitors, you are all working for common goals and fresh ideas help everyone involved."—*Promoter*

"We are stronger together! Be open-minded to collaborations. Outline specific goals and tasks, stay committed and constantly communicate."—*Protector*

"Personally—with a small staff—I love working with others outside of the organization. In general as an organization, we have grown because people feel more committed to a partnership vs. just being a member." —*Promoter*

CHAPTER 6

Communication in Collaborations

I am the daughter of an actor, writer, and director (my mother) and an entrepreneur (my father). When I was a little girl, if you asked me what I wanted to be when I grew up, I would often say, "an actor, just like my mom." Somewhere along the way, maybe around age eight, my answer changed to, "I want to be a business owner, just like my dad." More than forty years later, I find that my journey has merged these two professions. My personal desire to write this book came from my passion for business and entrepreneurship. The topic of this book was grounded in many experiences throughout my life, but I can trace the very foundation back to those earliest desires to be an actor. The very essence of the creative process that happens when producing theatre is grounded in collaboration. Imagine how complete strangers enter a rehearsal on day one and emerge weeks later with a finished performance, a work of art. Have you ever wondered what it really takes to make that happen?

Communication is key to making that creative collaborative process work. As I shared earlier, good implementation is founded in strategies for building transparency and a shared vision, establishing roles and goals, and creating a communication plan.

Those strategies are important, but the real power to success is in the soft skills. In other words, the way you show up to the collaboration will make the biggest impact. Let's look at the creative collaborative process a little closer. In an interview on Steve Farber's *Love is Just Damn Good Business* podcast, The Brothers Koren share their perspective on the art of collaboration. In that interview, the musicians talk about good ego and bad ego and what they call "daring to suck."

To hear more about The Brothers Koren:

Listen to the podcast:
https://nicolemahoney.com/stronger-together-resources

The Brothers Koren compare good and bad ego to good and bad fats. Good fats support a healthy diet while bad fats tend to stick around and cause negative health effects. Similarly, the good ego shows up for a healthy conversation and is prepared to share ideas without attachment to them. Meanwhile, the bad ego stays emotionally attached to the idea and wants to be sure the idea is used or liked. It is human nature to be emotionally attached to your ideas. The most powerful collaborations happen when people become conscious of the good and bad ego and choose to show up with the good one, without attachment. Another way to think about this according to The Brothers Koren is to *dare to suck*. Share your first creative idea freely without filtering it, let the idea be received, and accept that it may or may not be used. Daring to suck feeds the collaborative process and will lead to stronger teams and bigger ideas.

Another principle that can be helpful to productive and open communication among collaborators is one that has been used in improv for decades. The two words "yes, and" are a rule of thumb that is used in improvisational theater as a method of allowing the participant to accept what one actor is saying and expand on it to create a bigger idea. This same technique can be used when brainstorming with a collaborative team. One person shares an idea, and other participants accept that idea and expand on it without judgement. Adopting "yes, and" thinking will help you make sure you have brought your good ego to the collaboration.

Improving listening skills and asking high-gain questions will make you a better communicator and collaborator. In episode 231 of *Destination on the Left*, I interviewed keynote speaker and performance coach Carol Lempert. She is a trained actor who shares her performance secrets with executives to help them improve their presence and supercharge their careers. The ideas and techniques Lempert shared translate from her experience collaborating as an actor to business communications and leadership.

Your overall presence on the collaborative team is impacted by what your fellow collaborators hear and how you make them feel. What you say will reflect on your presence and can demonstrate your level of interest in the other person or the project you are collaborating on. Asking nonjudgmental questions that come from real curiosity will help you strengthen your presence. To start, when sharing ideas with your fellow collaborators, stay away from closed questions—those that can be answered with one word, often a yes or a no. Instead, ask open-ended questions that start with *what* or *how* to gain insight into the other person's point of view. Great open-ended questions to use in a collaboration include:

- What do you think?
- What have I missed?
- What are your thoughts?

To make even stronger connections, ask high-gain questions. These questions tell you something about the other person, they make the other person feel safe enough to share, and they provide a deeper understanding of the person's values and what is important to them. A few examples of high-gain questions are:

- Where in your career have you experienced a successful collaboration?
- When did you first learn how to collaborate, and what

was that experience like?

- What are the things that will hold people back?
- What are the things that people are missing?
- Who would want to visit my location/business?
- What can we build into our message that will entice people to take action?

High-gain questions enable you to listen more deeply and learn about your fellow collaborators. When you combine these questions with active listening, people will feel heard, engaged, and safe. You will find that people will frequently reveal what they value when sharing their point of view, and listening at a deeper level will help you understand what is important to the other person. Paraphrasing what you heard back to them will make them feel understood and acknowledged.

When working with others, disagreements are bound to happen. It is important to remember that disagreements are healthy and lead to building new ideas and solving problems. When we get stuck because of a disagreement, it's often because our values are in conflict. A technique to move past this is to acknowledge the other person's values and focus on the problem you are working on. Move the conversation off of the emotional and back to the problem you are solving together.

Listen to the full interview with Carol Lempert visit:
https://nicolemahoney.com/stronger-together-resources

Bringing your good ego, daring to suck, employing "yes, and" thinking, and asking high-gain questions are likely easier said than done. There are many things that can get in your way. One of the biggest obstacles that many people suffer from is imposter syndrome. It gets in our way every time we try to achieve something new.

You may be suffering from imposter syndrome too. You know the phenomena that happens when that little voice in your head tells you that your ideas aren't good enough. If you try this new thing, what if it doesn't work, or what if others don't agree with you? One of my podcast guests, Kris Kelso, author of *Overcoming The Imposter*, calls this the comparison trap, and he warns not to fall for it.

Kelso explains that imposter syndrome is about feeling like a fraud or feeling like you are not really a success despite evidence to the contrary. The comparison trap tricks you into measuring yourself against others. It is the measuring stick that says you are only adequate or legitimate if you can measure up to another person, another business, or another part of the industry, but this comparison is not reality; it is just a trap. Don't fall for it. Instead, Kelso encourages measuring success against ourselves instead of others. By measuring against your own goals, you will know well enough whether you are making progress, and what others have done becomes irrelevant. It doesn't matter whether it seems like you're keeping up or are falling behind. What matters is how you feel about your own progress toward what you are trying to achieve.

To learn more about imposter syndrome:

Listen to Kris Kelso's full interview at:
https://nicolemahoney.com/stronger-together-resources

I found a perfect example of what can be accomplished when you move past the comparison trap in my daughter Maeve when she was 18 years old. Maeve is the second child in our family to graduate high school, and three years before it was her turn, she attended her older sister's graduation. She was inspired by the student commencement speaker at that graduation and told me that she wanted to be the speaker at her graduation ceremony. Anyone who is a parent knows that sometimes kids change their minds, but Maeve did not. In our school district, it is not the smartest kids who get to speak. We don't have a valedictorian or salutatorian like many other districts. Commencement speakers are chosen from a panel of teachers and students through an audition process.

When the auditions came up in the spring of Maeve's senior year, she started to think that she wasn't good enough and that maybe she shouldn't audition because there were so many kids who were better speakers, students, you name it—all better than her. I quickly told her there was one way to be sure she wouldn't get picked, and that was not even to try. That must have sunk in because Maeve did try out, and she was one of two selected to give the commencement addresses. Maeve heard the little voices in the back of her head telling her not to try, and she still went for it anyway.

Watch for the comparison trap, and don't let imposter syndrome stop you from showing up to a collaboration ready to make an impact.

Another key to having successful communication in collaboration is showing up with the right mindset. When you adopt a *growth mindset*, you view everything as an opportunity to learn, grow, and expand. However, those who adopt a *fixed mindset* believe they only have a set amount of capabilities and can only operate in a certain way, and they get stopped in their tracks by challenges. Having a growth mindset can make all the difference in how you communicate and contribute.

I explored this concept with Michelle Carlen from Alignment Advising on my podcast episode 219. Carlen spoke about the importance of communication in leadership and pointed out that being open-minded provides you with the opportunity to learn from every interaction. According to Carlen, being open-minded means remembering that we don't know it all, and when you think you do, that's the red flag that indicates you may be falling into a fixed mindset. Leaning on a growth mindset allows you to accept that you don't know what you don't know and opens you up to new ideas.

> **Learn more from Michelle Carlen at:**
> https://nicolemahoney.com/stronger-together-resources

One way to master this thinking is to make engaging the growth mindset a conscious choice every day. When I was in my early thirties, Seran Wilkie, my life coach, gave me the following affirmation that I have read every morning since:

Today I will remember that
I do not know "everything" yet.
I will entertain the possibility that
everything is perfect
as it is for the moment.

This affirmation helps me acknowledge that I still have a lot to learn, and by accepting that everything is perfect in this moment, I open myself up to the possibilities of the next. In other words, I am not allowing imposter syndrome to creep in, I am staying in a growth mindset, and I am willing to dare to suck because I do not know what will happen when I share my idea with the world.

The Destination BC Story

In a conversation I had with Marsha Walden, formerly from Destination BC and currently the head of Destination Canada, on podcast episode 165, I found out exactly what is possible when communication is used to build collaboration. A lifelong British Columbian, Walden's career spans corporate leadership roles in marketing, strategy, transformation, operations, communications, and social responsibility. In our conversation, Walden acknowledged that working collaboratively is more difficult than going it alone. She references the old proverb that states, "If you want to go fast, go alone, but if you want to go far, go together." That is exactly the guiding principle that she leads with, and she shares four examples of how this has brought more success to Destination BC.

Example 1: Collaborative Culture

Walden was recruited to Destination British Columbia because the organization's board of directors saw her combined experience in operations transformation and marketing as exactly what they were looking for at the time. Her background leading different kinds of organizations prepared her for a position she calls a "CEO of people leadership." Walden views strategy and culture as her core functions. Strategy defines how an organization is going to win in the marketplace, and culture will foster the most engaged and motivated workforce in order to make great things happen through that strategy. Collaboration is core to Destination BC's strategy. They have created a culture of collaboration extending the concept beyond just words and truly embracing it as actions. One way that Destination BC puts collaboration into action is by giving the industry a voice in how the programs they develop come to life. This voice starts with a marketing committee of twenty members from around the province, all providing input. The organization uses high-gain questions when contemplating a big change, asking the industry what they think of the change, and seeking ways it could be made better. They review all of their programs every three years and solicit input from the industry on how they are doing and where they can improve.

Example 2: Ten-Year Destination Plans

Determining what you want your destination to be known

for requires a lot of collaboration. So out of a necessity to grow, Destination BC invited new parties—municipal governments, tourism businesses, industry stakeholders, indigenous nations, and other governmental organizations—to the table to establish a strategy. But these things take time, so Walden and her team operated under ten-year plans that allowed for realistic timelines to hit their goals.

British Columbia is about the same size as Washington, Oregon, and California combined. With such a vast area to sell to audiences, Destination BC created twenty planning areas to facilitate community-based conversations about what they wanted to be famous for and how the infrastructure needed to improve for travel and tourism experiences.

From these ten-year strategies, Destination BC set action plans over three-year horizons, which helped them put collaboration into action. The three-year tasks allow them to focus on things like improving transportation access in particular corridors to enhance connectivity, improving internet access in remote areas of the province, creating policy and incentive programs that address hotel shortages in some parts of the province, and working with national and provincial parks to ensure that they have the right number of campsites. A specific to-do list will improve the experience for all the province's visitors, including locals who travel close to home.

Maintaining momentum is an important component of keeping plans alive. It's critical to continually engage stakeholders that made input to the plans to demonstrate that their investment of time and ideas was a worthwhile exercise because it leads to real outcomes that are going to impact the success of their business and community over time. To mark their progress, Destination BC created dashboards that provide a baseline for where they started and will offer a continuous report over the next ten years.

Example 3: Content Commonwealth

Destination BC has been successful at sharing content, both user-generated and proprietary. To help the organization have the right content at the right time for the right message, they developed a content commonwealth. More than forty communities contribute to the content commonwealth, providing access to thousands of pieces of content for digital marketing. This content bank gives the destination an advantage for personalizing messages and making them more relevant to the consumer.

With a culture of collaboration, it makes sense that they consider all the tourism entities in the province as one enterprise with shared capabilities versus a group of independents working in silos. They believe the content commonwealth will be a distinct competitive advantage going forward, especially in the digital world.

Example 4: Marketing Partnerships

Destination BC recognized that bringing several communities along the same travel route together would encourage longer stays, provide a more compelling value proposition, and give communities a greater share of voice. It also allowed them to develop the overall travel experience and market it collectively. Destination BC works with roughly sixty different consortia of communities and sector groups across the province. They provide an investment-matching fund for collaborations that share common interests and marketing goals.

When they opened up the co-op marketing partnership program to other sectors, new collaborations were formed around themes such as fishing, skiing, mountain biking, and craft beer. The craft brewery industry, for example, decided that they wanted to access the co-op marketing fund. Sixteen craft breweries worked together to create the British Columbia Ale Trail, and they were awarded a matching investment from the fund. Three years later, the Ale Trail had 173 craft breweries featured in sixteen different self-guided mini-trails around the province. By organizing the sector around trails, visitors interested in craft beer are motivated to visit multiple communities. The BC Ale Trail also gives the collective group a louder voice and a compelling story.

To listen to the full podcast episode visit:
https://nicolemahoney.com/stronger-together-resources

CHAPTER 7

Commonality is Key

In 1987, I worked for my father's retail electronics store. The business started in the '70s selling and installing CB radios, which eventually led to aftermarket AM/FM radio/cassette players and other car audio components. By 1987, our store was one of the only places in western New York that could install mobile phones in automobiles, and business started booming. Suddenly, my father's business went from $1 million to $5 million a year in sales as his clientele changed from gearheads and truckers to professionals and business owners. As a smart entrepreneur and marketer, my father recognized the changing demographics of his customers and began to adapt and make rapid improvements to the overall customer experience. One of the marketing tactics that helped create loyalty and inspire repeat business was the personal touch of sending thank you and birthday cards to every customer. The cards included generous offers and coupons from my father's store and other local businesses who served a common audience demographic. My father approached other businesses by offering to include a coupon in every card he sent to his customers provided the other businesses furnished a substantial coupon. They gave him coupons for a free car wash, $10 off a meal at a local restaurant, and $25 off a purchase at a local jewelry store, among others. During my father's business boom, we were sending as many as 10,000 cards out per month. This is where the idea of collaborating with others who share something in common started taking shape for me.

Successful collaborations start with commonality. The most important elements in finding it include establishing and agreeing on goals, having strong champions, and designing the collaboration to benefit all participants.

Establishing and Agreeing on Goals

Prior to seeking collaborative partnerships, you must identify the goals you want to accomplish. I like to follow the SMART goal format—goals should be specific, measurable, attainable, relevant, and time-based.

A SMART goal for my father's retail store, for example,

would have been to increase customer loyalty and repeat purchases through a thank you and birthday card program that provides huge value.

This is how the SMART goal format applies.

Specific—*What exactly will you accomplish?* Build loyalty and repeat purchases with existing customers through a thank you and birthday card program.

Measurable—*How will you know when you have reached this goal?* We could measure our customer loyalty through repeat sales. Our collaborative partners could measure the outcomes of the goal through redemption of coupons and new customer acquisition.

Attainable—*Is achieving this goal realistic with effort and commitment? Have you got the resources to achieve this goal? If not, how will you get them?* We had the mailing list, data, budget, and labor needed to prepare and mail each thank you and birthday card. We needed to go out and get partners to provide value-adds to include in them.

Relevant—*Why is this goal significant to your business, to society, to your industry, or to your customers?* The goal was relevant to the customer because it provided them with another connection to the business while introducing them to other local businesses through generous coupon offers. It was relevant to our collaborators because we shared common target audiences and it helped bring them new customers.

Time-based—*When will you achieve this goal?* This

goal was established as an ongoing initiative that occurred monthly.

Once you establish your SMART goal, answer these additional questions:

- Why is this goal important?
- What are the benefits of achieving it?
- What are the potential obstacles?
- What are the possible solutions to the obstacles?
- Who are the people you will ask to help you achieve the goal?
- What steps need to be taken to achieve the goal?

Being clear on your goals will help you seek out the right partners for your collaboration. As Tony Robbins says, "Setting goals is the first step in turning the invisible into the visible." In other words, knowing what you want to accomplish is the first step in being able to make the accomplishment real not only to yourself but to others who will want to join you as well.

Strong Champions Make Strong Partners

Having strong champions for a collaboration, not only those who are leading it but also those who rally around it and "sell it" to others, is essential to success.

I found a perfect example of "strong champions making stronger partners" when I interviewed Heather Bagshaw, Former Tourism Director for Greene County and the Northern

Catskills on my podcast episode 218.

On the night of March 16, 2020, the last night before the state of New York mandated closure of businesses, Bagshaw had planned to go out to dinner to get a burger with friends. While she was there, she spoke with the restaurant owner and listened to them as they shared concerns about the uncertainty ahead. It was the day before St. Patrick's Day, and they had prepared for what was traditionally a big night. There were worries about what to do with the inventory and long-term worries about how to survive a closure. Heather then went next door to a local pub, where she found three other restaurant owners in conversation, trying to figure out what to do. One of them, a single mom, was crying because she was worried about providing for her family and the unknown hit her hard.

Listening to these stories, Heather felt the need to do something. After a sleepless night, she got on the phone with her marketing agency, shared the stories, and told them she wanted to do something for the restaurants, but she wasn't sure what. Over the next twenty-four hours, Heather and her team reached out to every single restaurant in the county to find out what their plans were and how her office could help. They collected data and kept a detailed spreadsheet of what each restaurant was offering for takeout, curbside service, delivery, breakfast, lunch, or dinner. Then the Takeout in Greene campaign was born. Almost overnight, the tourism office developed a website and started a radio and social media campaign which launched later that month and ran through September 2020.

Out of this grew a community and an outlet for the restaurants throughout the county to take a step back and focus on working together to get through the crisis. Many of them got creative. Some started offering dinner packages instead of one-off meals, a lot of them re-did their websites and added online ordering, and others offered delivery service and the ability to have drinks to go. It wasn't just what the tourism office did that helped them, it's what the collective effort did to move all of them forward.

This turned out to be a perfect case study for collaboration. In addition to the restaurants, the tourism office worked closely with the Chamber of Commerce, the economic development office, and the local radio station to pull this off. There were many champions of the collective goals in this story, and they turned out to be strong partners, proving that a rising tide truly does lift all boats.

This is a story of co-opetition that helped local restaurants survive during the pandemic. COVID-19 pushed the Greene County tourism office to look internally at what they provided for the small towns and local businesses that make up the larger community.

Commonality can be found when you have common goals, but it can also be found when you face a common challenge. Sometimes, it takes a crisis to show us how important collaborating with those we normally perceive as competitors really is to mutual success.

To listen to Heather Bagshaw's full interview, visit:
https://nicolemahoney.com/stronger-together-resources

Collaborations Benefit All Participants

When you find commonality and clearly communicate your goals, collaborations can be designed to benefit everyone involved. A good illustration of how this works can be found on my podcast episode 186, when we learned about the "Staten Island shuffle" and how a collaboration between competitors led to more opportunity for everyone involved.

The Staten Island Ferry is a passenger ferry operated by the New York City Department of Transportation. This free ferry offers some of the best views of the Manhattan skyline, the Statue of Liberty, and Ellis Island. The ride is very popular among the millions of visitors who go to NYC each year. Sightseers ride the ferry to Staten Island, get off, and get back on the next ferry back to Manhattan. Colleen Siuzdak from Visit Staten Island calls this the "Staten Island shuffle." The challenge was getting visitors to stay in Staten Island and enjoy the cultural attractions, outdoor experiences, and businesses found there before returning to Manhattan.

Visit Staten Island decided to position the ferry as the front door to the destination, aimed at reframing the ferry from a commuter boat to a fun, free, and exciting sightseeing experience. Beyond that, they wanted riders of the ferry to realize it was a doorway, an extension to the Manhattan experience that offered something unique and memorable.

With this idea in mind, Visit Staten Island reached out to other partners with common interests and created a collaborative branding effort. They engaged with the Staten Island Chamber of Commerce, Empire State Development, and Destination St. George on a collaborative branding project that led to the creation of a new brand under the tagline "The Unexpected Borough." The new brand gave the destination a common framework for their positioning with the message, "If you haven't seen Staten Island, the unexpected borough, you haven't actually seen NYC."

Armed with new brand messaging and the goal of getting more visitors to spend time in Staten Island, Sziudak joined Jennifer Sammartino, another leader with Visit Staten Island, and reached across the New York Harbor looking for a partnership that could help them move closer to their goal. They approached the Downtown Alliance in Manhattan, an organization that manages the Downtown-Lower Manhattan Business Improvement District (BID), the part of Manhattan from which the Staten Island Ferry departs. Sziudak and Sammartino were not sure that the Downtown Alliance would be open to working with them because Visit Staten Island was a much smaller organization. Sammartino used the phrase "small potatoes," comparing their organization to the Manhattan Downtown Alliance. To their surprise, they learned Staten Island shared a common problem with the Downtown Alliance—both were trying to enhance the visitor experience and serve the visiting public. They found out that roughly 30 percent of visitors who were embarking on the Staten Island Ferry wanted to know what there was to do on

Staten Island. Visitor services for the Downtown Alliance would field these questions daily and had little knowledge about Staten Island, feeling unable to do their jobs.

As a result of this new collaboration, Visit Staten Island invested in digital advertising for all the amazing things there are to do on Staten Island at the Whitehall Ferry Terminal, the point of departure for the ferry. They also started a brochure exchange with the Downtown Alliance, placing their brochures at Manhattan visitor centers and placing Manhattan brochures at Staten Island visitor centers. Not only did Visit Staten Island solve the problem of the Staten Island shuffle by getting information into the hands of visitors, they also enhanced the visitor experience by extending the NYC experience beyond Manhattan and onto the island.

For additional details, listen to the full interview with Colleen Siuzdak and Jennifer Sammartino:

To listen to the full interview, visit:
https://nicolemahoney.com/stronger-together-resources

CHAPTER 8

Commitment Leads to Success

Successful collaborations rely on the commitment of all parties to the project. With commitment in the mix, everyone shares in the success and will see it through. When a firefighter runs into a burning house, they are committed to seeing that fire extinguished, and all of their collaborators (the other firefighters) are just as committed to the success of the mission.

The story of the Autism Nature Trail (ANT) at Letchworth State Park demonstrates the power of commitment in business collaboration. This project had a goal of creating a one-mile loop trail within a New York State Park that featured eight unique outdoor sensory stations meant to stimulate growth and a sense of inclusivity for those with autism spectrum disorder and other developmental disabilities.

The Public-Private Partnership supporting the campaign to build the autism nature trail at Letchworth State Park included the Natural Heritage Trust, Perry Central School District, Letchworth State Park, and the New York State Office of Parks, Recreation, and Historic Preservation, all of whom were committed to the success of the project. The project was seen as a way to engage the local community and local schools in providing access to nature for an underserved audience. It also served as an engine for regional economic growth, development, and tourism. The partnership was also supported by Camp Puzzle Peace, a Rochester based not-for-profit organization pioneering outdoor recreational opportunities for individuals with ASD and their families, which was tasked to provide on-site programs for the trail.

For three years prior to January 2020, the ANT was in a silent phase of fundraising for $2 million and was ready to launch into the public portion of its capital campaign. The goal was to raise the remaining $1.9 million needed to fund construction and operations of the trail throughout the year 2020 and begin groundbreaking in early 2021.

Two short months into the public fundraising push, the effects of COVID-19 landed swiftly. With many in the community facing financial burden and uncertainty, and with in-person events being shuttered keeping major donors away, the ANT needed leadership to rise to the challenge and find ways to support the community while raising the final funds for its project.

The collaborative partners decided to make a donor newsletter the main communication channel and that updates on the project would be announced to past and potential donors and ongoing supporters. The newsletter was released bi-weekly with content focused on major milestones and news, opportunities to give, the delivery of an "About the ANT" video series, and a special Donor Spotlight featuring companies and individuals giving to the project in unique or creative ways.

Social media was another major platform the company used to reach new people and build awareness for the project. In April 2020, the ANT was announced as part of a March Madness-style bracket contest hosted by a regional business, Cellino Plumbing & HVAC. Competing against sixty-two other area non-profits, the ANT was tasked with encouraging their supporters to vote once per day to help the project move up the brackets and win a donation of almost $10,000 and have a Cellino Truck wrapped in their unique project branding. Using social media as the main channel to spread the word, the ANT won the contest, the money, and the local publicity.

Local and regional public relations helped the ANT spread the word about its campaign across upstate New York. Instead of focusing on a donor message, the collaborative partners looked for feel-good stories about the project. At a time when the news was often focused on the negative effects of the COVID-19 pandemic, the ANT team wanted to be the light in the darkness by focusing on the good in the community.

Press releases focused on messages of nature and the healing qualities of fresh air, the members of the autism spectrum community that would benefit from the trail, and sharing ways that the ANT would give back through programming and partnerships with the Perry Central School District and Camp Puzzle Peace.

In the fall of 2020, restrictions had lifted enough for the team to hold an in-person VIP donor event in Letchworth State Park. A small group gathering of twenty-five people was planned in the Humphrey Nature Center, the building adjacent to the future site of the ANT, with a short indoor presentation followed by a VIP tour of the trail. The event was live-streamed on Facebook, providing access to many who would have been otherwise unable to attend. A special video presentation was shared at the event, with more than forty individual clips from supporters sharing their readiness and need for the project.

Throughout the campaign, the team continued to seek out ways to build support for the project and drive awareness of this new endeavor among community members. An online silent auction of donated items and special experiences called "The ANT Experience" drove donations in the fall. A partnership with a local photographer sparked a GoFundMe calendar campaign which resulted in another $20,100 donated to the trail. Even major celebrities shared their support, with actor Joe Mantegna filming a video for the project thanking supporters after sharing the impact this project could have for his own daughter, who has autism.

One supporter signed her entire stimulus payment over

to the ANT project, and a small business donated a portion of their May proceeds to the project as word spread about their services.

Most importantly, through the commitment to the collaborative effort, the Autism Nature Trail raised $1.9 million dollars over the course of ten months, completing its public fundraising initiative and paving the way for a spring 2021 groundbreaking.

The partners involved with the ANT all felt accountable to their contributions, had a well-informed leadership team, and exhibited full commitment by all partners. This commitment to the collaboration proved that when there is a will, there is a way, and despite a pandemic, they were able to see their project through to the end.

> To listen to Loren Penman's interview visit:
> https://nicolemahoney.com/stronger-together-resources

Obstacles to Commitment

It's not easy to stay committed to a collaboration as many things can stand in the way. Even without a pandemic, the lack of funding or human resources, a lack of leadership support, competing priorities, or a lack of trust can drive a wedge between collaborators and diminish success.

Lack of Funding or Other Resources

When a lack of resources became an issue for communities

in the Dingle Peninsula, they turned to building relationships and collaboration to overcome that obstacle.

The Dingle Peninsula Tourism Alliance was formed as a marketing cooperative owned and managed by its members across the peninsula. It's a non-profit organization dedicated to the development and promotion of tourism, and it's run by committee. The tourism alliance represents a cross-section of the area businesses, communities, and committees providing an inclusive approach to every group and business operating on the Dingle Peninsula, both directly and indirectly involved in tourism. Some of the organization's key aims are to support local businesses in a sustainable way, support the growth of jobs in existing and new businesses, extend the season with an increase in overnight visitation, and sustain communities and families in the villages and towns along the Dingle Peninsula.

When I talked to Caroline Boland and Gary Curran from the tourism alliance, they pointed to a number of important relationships that were enabling the success of the collaboration.

First, they actively built relationships with the nine villages and communities across the peninsula. From the very beginning, it was important for the organization to have buy-in and engagement from all areas. It took feet on the ground to build these relationships by visiting each community to find out what the needs were, where the pressure points were, and what ideas each had for the future. Then they continued the conversation with monthly meetings to discuss the vision for the tourism alliance and how it could best serve the collective good. This is a terrific example of successfully building a collaboration by gaining commitment to an overarching vision. The real achievement was getting everyone to come together, tapping into their collective thinking to arrive at a single shared vision. Through regular meetings and reporting, everyone involved was engaged, committed, and moving toward that vision.

Boland and Curran recognized that the organization needed to take a grassroots approach to reaching new visitor markets. With a limited budget, they wanted to make sure every dollar spent was delivering more than a dollar back to the peninsula. The second relationship they sought to forge was with their sister city, Springfield, Massachusetts. Recognizing that Irish heritage runs deep in this city, they wanted to tap into that heritage and explore ways to collaborate with the City beyond the ceremonial sign and dignitary trip.

When Boland and Curran were in the United States for a travel bloggers conference, they added a trip to Western Massachusetts. They learned that throughout history, the success of the Dingle Peninsula relied on relationships. You don't have to have money to make new friends. You just have to be genuine, welcoming, and willing to spend time building relationships. Recognizing that the relationship with the greater Springfield area goes back hundreds of years, Boland and Curran wanted to celebrate, respect, maintain, and develop it.

On this first trip to Springfield, Boland and Curran had an opportunity to spend a number of days meeting and visiting with the Mayor of Springfield, the local tourism organization, local high school, local college, and the Eastern

States Exposition—home of the Big E, one of the top ten Fairs in North America and the largest on the East Coast. They used the visit to explore joint opportunities that had the potential to grow and make a real difference.

A lack of resources does not have to be an obstacle to collaboration. Like Boland and Curran found out, you can forge a relationship with your sister city by seeing it for the opportunity it is, by getting to know the people there and building those relationships organically, and by getting the folks in Springfield to spread the message about the Dingle Peninsula. Caroline Boland and Gary Curra share their story:

To listen to the interview:
https://nicolemahoney.com/stronger-together-resources

Lack of Leadership Support

Every project needs a champion, and in the case of a collaboration, it may need many. Champions constantly sing the praises of the collaboration, share the successes, and provide updates to others in their organization. Champions keep the collaboration front and center with leadership or other stakeholders.

When Jennifer Wesselhoff was CEO and President of the Sedona Chamber of Commerce and Tourism Bureau, she led the development of Arizona's first Sustainable Tourism Plan and saw tourism grow to become Sedona's largest industry with a $1 billion annual impact and 10,000 tourism-related jobs.

Wesselhoff was the biggest cheerleader for tourism in her area, and in order to commit to a sustainable tourism plan, she first had to recognize the trade-offs of the industry.

She started by listening to the complaints of residents who didn't like traffic congestion, trail head parking overflowing into neighborhoods, the impact of short-term rentals on the character of neighborhoods, or the noise created by helicopter tours. She recognized that as a cheerleader for the tourism industry, her reflexive response to these complaints would be, "Yeah, but did you know that tourism generates 70 percent of our sales taxes, that 10,000 people rely on tourism jobs, or that we don't have a property tax because of tourism?"

What she once thought were just inconveniences or trade-offs for having a robust tourism economy were now starting to become stressors on fragile environments and ecosystems. She recognized that destinations with these stressors, especially ones in rural communities which may lie next to national or state parks, open space, or public land, were dealing with these issues and trying to answer the question, "How much is too much?" The journey toward sustainable tourism began with a new lens focused on how to mitigate the negative impacts of tourism by recognizing all of the trade-offs.

The process of sustainable tourism management in Sedona started with defining it as a balance between creating and retaining a vibrant economy, providing a positive visitor experience against the impacts tourism has on quality of life for residents, and protecting the environment.

With a shared definition, Wesselhoff became a champion for the sustainable planning process which led to a comprehensive community-wide collaboration designed to identify the role that tourism plays in sustainability. Sedona took a data-driven approach by starting with a benchmarking process to figure out just how sustainable they were as a destination. They brought in an outside consultant through the Global Sustainable Tourism Council to conduct a destination assessment. This process brought in key community stakeholders including policymakers.

They learned through the destination assessment that there were many different groups, non-profits, and organizations who were doing great things in the community, but independently. This prevented them from having a shared vision they could all work toward collaboratively.

A key component of the sustainable tourism plan was trying to align residents with three audiences: businesses, non-profits, and land managers. Wesselhoff noted her organization was good at talking to the businesses, their members, and their stakeholders. They were good at talking to visitors and finding out what they liked and wanted more or less of, but they typically weren't so great at talking to residents about their feelings related to the future of tourism.

Planning for sustainable tourism in Sedona became a wide collaboration in the community designed to get everyone aligned and moving in the same direction. The planning collaboration was far-reaching, and the group leaned on the definition that was established at the beginning to stay focused. They reached out to the non-profits who had a mission, vision, or values that aligned with protecting the environment. One of the hardest parts was staying focused and not letting the project get too big or stray from tourism. The collaborative planning committee knew they were designing an initiative with the purpose of identifying tourism's role in sustainability and not a broader community sustainable plan. They needed to test every goal, objective, or tactic against the tourism lens. They recognized that governmental agencies have a bigger vision of sustainability and can take a broader look at things like a community-wide climate action plan. That isn't the role of the sustainable tourism plan.

Through this process, the Sedona tourism industry learned to use the power of their influence to educate businesses and change how they behave in relation to sustainable tourism. They also learned how to influence the visitor once they arrived in the community. By playing a stronger role in impacting visitor behavior, the organization could help improve the quality of life for residents while also protecting the environment. For example, by helping visitors ride transit or establishing walkability programs, they eliminated some cars from the road, which led to less traffic and congestion. Introducing Leave No Trace programs in parks and trails or dispersing visitors away from popular trails and helping them find the hidden gems that have more capacity to accommodate visitors also improved quality of life and alleviated some of the complaints residents shared.

Listen to Jennifer Wesselhoff's full interview:
https://nicolemahoney.com/stronger-together-resources

Competing Priorities

Commitment to a collaboration can get sidelined when external forces impact an organization and cause a shift in priorities to individual needs. I recently stumbled upon some research done on the underground networks of forests. I have a cursory interest in trees since my husband is a forester. This research, to my surprise, had relevance to my study of collaboration, and it specifically supports the prioritization of the needs of a population over the needs of an individual. The research conducted by Suzanne Simard, a professor in the Department of Forest and Conservation at the University of British Columbia, showed that old-growth forests rely on an entire ecosystem of trees, undergrowth plants, fungi, and microbes to survive. They work together as a superorganism in a symbiotic way, connected, communicative, and co-dependent. This struck me as another example of how important collaboration is to survival.

This is an interesting twist on what scientists have long believed to be the emphasis of the individual. Darwin's theory of natural selection stated that all living creatures were locked into a contest for limited resources, and that the needs of the individual would win out over the needs of the whole. In Sinard's research, there is a greater focus on cooperation over self-interest and on the living system over just one unit. She found that while there is conflict in forests for resources, there is also negotiation and reciprocity. In other words, the whole is greater than the sum of its parts. When external forces put pressure on the individual, cooperation among the collective can help one population outcompete another—an altruistic forest community outlasting a selfish one, for example.

Travel Alliance Partners, a partner-owned corporation, was created in 2002 as an innovative way to help tour operators grow their businesses. At the time of its forming, the tour business was suffering due to a post-9/11 lag in the economy. The business owners who founded the corporation thought they would have a better chance at filling their tour departures if they partnered with their competitors from other markets to help sell them. This ultimately gave each of the tour operator partners more product to sell without the cost or time it took to develop the product, and it provided exposure to new audiences they may not have otherwise been able to reach. As the organization grew over the next decade, they applied their collaborative approach to working with suppliers in the industry. They recognized the importance of establishing and maintaining deep relationships with hotels, restaurants, attractions, destinations, and service providers they relied on to produce their tours.

One way they accomplished this was through their annual conference, TAP Dance, which I mentioned earlier in this book. This event is a preferred conference for many travel professionals because of its relaxed environment, long-standing relationships, and proven format designed to impact business growth for TAP Tour Operators and their suppliers.

In 2020, faced with travel restrictions and dramatically reduced budgets due to the COVID-19 pandemic, TAP needed to quickly develop an event that would replace their on-site conference. Despite mandates not to meet in person, the event still required the personal and interactive elements associated with the TAP brand. At a time when external forces were creating an uncertain future, it was more important than ever to rely on the collaborations that TAP provided to help everyone survive. Holding a conference in June 2020 despite the obstacles continued the TAP tradition of being an innovative leader in the travel, tourism, and hospitality industries. They demonstrated their commitment to the partnerships necessary for success in the industry.

With more than 500 private virtual meetings, hundreds of attendees, entertaining videos, international guests, and fun virtual activities, the event was a welcome reprieve from the distance that the pandemic had put between people who are used to seeing one another every year.

While the 2020 virtual event exceeded expectations, committing to another virtual conference in 2021 was unexpected, but necessary. Between tours no longer running, budget cutbacks, and furloughed staff, TAP recognized that the need for collaboration with other industry professionals was more important than ever to recover and grow business.

People still longed for a sense of connection, to maintain critical relationships, and to share not only current struggles but learn how to lean into one another to move forward. "Rebuilding together" was the common thread that connected the TAP network, and TAP Dance was a way for the group to stay committed, motivated, and supportive. There was light at the end of the tunnel, and once it was within reach, pent-up demand for travel would soar, and this group would be ready.

TAP took on the challenge of reinventing its virtual TAP Dance to again ensure it offered the best value and exciting opportunities for suppliers that would strategically fit into navigating the world's tumultuous times. Collaborate, motivate, and innovate became the words that thoughtfully inspired them to reimagine the event format.

Everyone in the TAP network needed travelers. Tour operators needed departures, destination suppliers needed visitors, and travel buyers needed clients. With travel at a halt, TAP recognized the immediate need to "get ready to be ready." This meant going beyond bringing like-minded audiences together for a typical TAP Dance, but instead, rolling out a new collection of travel products under the Ignite Travel Collection, a curated group of tours designed to get everyone traveling again with inspiring packages—whether off-the-beaten path getaways or bucket list trips.

At the second virtual Tap Dance, a hundred attendees worked together to create eighteen new travel products that were rolled out and launched to 250 travel buyers under the Ignite Travel Collection umbrella. Cooperation is what helped TAP tour operator partners and their suppliers survive the external forces that COVID-19 presented.

Importance of Trust

When trust exists within a collaboration, your commitment to the project becomes stronger. Trust provides for a safe environment where ideas can be shared and built upon freely. It gives fellow collaborators the confidence to open themselves up to collaboration and fosters an atmosphere that encourages communication. When trust exists among a collaborative group, everyone involved assumes positive intent, which feeds innovation and creativity and supports faster decision-making.

For episode 123 of *Destination on the Left*, I talked with Jason Murray about his experience building an adventure tour operation from scratch. With tours running all over the southwestern United States, it is all about trust and relationship-building. From customers to guides to all those involved with making these unique experiences happen, building relationships and trust has been the key to Murray's success.

As a native of Utah, Murray grew up visiting national parks, monuments, and other regions throughout the American West. He has enjoyed camping, hiking, backpacking, and touring throughout the region for decades. One of his greatest loves is sharing his passion for the history, geology, and beauty of the southwest with the tours he hosts through his company, Southwest Adventure Tours.

As a tour operator, Murray relies on destination marketing organizations for information and broader marketing initiatives to attract clients to his offerings. He relies on service providers like river rafting companies and glamping outfitters—providers who could easily undercut him and steal customers away. It all comes down to trust. That is why developing relationships is important, from customers to all the players in the travel ecosystem. When you know and trust each other, the opportunity to cooperate gives everyone a fair shake. Wrestling for the same clientele can be nerve-wracking, but you have to put yourself out there and find the people and organizations that are a good fit. Trusting his partners and building long-lasting relationships have helped Murray grow his company to a multi-million-dollar operation.

Successful collaborations start with trust. Knowing your fellow collaborators have your back and you are all in it for the greater good will lead to a deeper commitment and ultimately better collaborations.

> To listen to Jason Murray's full interview visit:
> https://nicolemahoney.com/stronger-together-resources

CHAPTER 9

The Key to Improving Diversity, Equity, and Inclusion

It should go without saying, but we must—collaborations will be more successful if we build our teams to be more diverse, equitable, and inclusive. Further, collaboration itself is the key to helping our industry solve issues related to DEI. By its very nature, collaboration leads to greater diversity. By partnering with other organizations and different types of collaborators, you will open yourself up to new perspectives and different opportunities. The more backgrounds and points of view involved in a collaboration, the more effective it will be.

According to the 2021 Collaboration Impact study, 50 percent of respondents said that the teams they've collaborated with have been very diverse in terms of experience with collaboration and the level of their roles in their organization. Strikingly, only 14 percent of respondents said their collaborative teams have been diverse with respect to race or culture. In this, collaborating teams are woefully lacking. Additionally, when respondents were asked if they believed that inter-organizational collaboration could help organizations in the travel, tourism, and hospitality industry survive current challenges and be more successful over the next five years, 60 percent of respondents overall and 81 percent of Promoters answered "definitely." Doubters and Protectors were more reserved, but nearly half of each of these segments still responded "definitely."

Recent social unrest has focused new attention on issues of diversity, equity, and inclusion as organizations and industries reflect on where they stand and how they measure up. For my company, equity is one of our core values, and in 2020, my team decided to lean into it. We began by evaluating how we were living up to the value and identifying where we could improve. What followed was a series of small steps that led to our company's prioritization of diversity, equity, and inclusion.

Growth-mindedness is another core value at our company, making it natural for us to seek out learning opportunities to help expand our understanding of diversity, equity, and inclusion. The team participated in a 21-day racial equity challenge hosted by the local United Way, attended implicit bias training hosted by the Society of American Travel Writers, and attended the Travel Unity Summit. We reflected as a team on what we learned and found these takeaways, which can also help to improve collaborations:

1. Embrace humility and vulnerability when addressing biases and issues related to diversity, equity, and inclusion.

2. Understand the difference between empathy and sympathy. Empathy is the ability to understand and share the feelings of another while sympathy is a feeling of pity and sorrow for someone else's misfortune. To be truly inclusive, we need to have empathy for others. Being empathetic allows us to have a deeper connection with others. Empathy does not involve judgement; instead, it allows us to acknowledge others' feelings and to discover their perspective.

3. Diversity without inclusion or equity can result in tokenism. In other words, if all one wants to accomplish is diversity, then one may only make a symbolic effort to keep up appearances. We have all heard the phrase, *"the token (insert underrepresented group here) in the room."* When you consider efforts to be inclusive—that is, not excluding anyone—and add dedication to being equitable—that is, giving everyone the same chance to participate—the dynamics change.

4. Equity and equality are not the same. Equality means everyone gets the same thing, but equity means everyone gets a different thing in proportion to the same need. To illustrate this point, imagine a family of four—a mother, a father, a thirteen-year-old son, and an eight-year-old daughter—who all want to ride bikes together. If the family valued equality among its members, everyone would get the same exact bike. They would be the same height, have the same seat, the same configuration, the same number of wheels. Can you imagine all four of these family members using the same model? Some would have a comfortable, easy ride, while others would either struggle or not be able to ride at all because the bike didn't fit their needs. Conversely, if the family valued equity, they would make sure everyone got the bike that best suited their needs so that everyone could experience the same ride.

One thing we identified when digging into our core value of equity is that our team was not diverse enough. We recognized that we had religious and age diversity, but that's where it stopped. Since we were not hiring in 2020, we decided to look at our partners, suppliers, and sub-contractors. We wanted different perspectives, so we intentionally sought out more diverse subcontractors to add to our team. Through this process, we added more diversity to our freelance team and engaged with them on client projects. We did not reserve the freelance bench for projects aligned with their background. Instead, we integrated them into our team and brought their diverse perspectives to the projects that were already in place.

To build a more diverse collaboration, be intentional about the partners you seek. Look for those who bring different perspectives to the table. Setting your intentions and focusing will lead you toward achieving your goals. When you set an intention and start to act, things happen. They may seem like small, incremental moves at first, but suddenly you will find yourself reflecting and notice how those incremental moves have led to monumental shifts and changes.

Historical Figure brings DEI to the Forefront: Auburn, NY

Harriet Tubman's chosen hometown is Auburn, NY, located in Cayuga County in part of the Finger Lakes vacation region of New York State. When Cayuga County Tourism Director Karen Kuhl found out that the 200th anniversary of Tubman's birthday was happening in 2022, she saw an opportunity to reposition her county in the minds of its visitors and residents alike, and she planned to accomplish this through a far-reaching collaboration. Kuhl saw the modern relevance of a historical product and leveraged that to focus her rural community on diversity, equity, and inclusion.

Harriet Tubman is internationally recognized as a symbol of freedom. After escaping from slavery, she owned property, built a farm, and was laid to rest in Auburn. Kuhl describes Harriet Tubman's link to Auburn as a hidden gem because the product, story, and linkages had not been fully developed. Located in the community were her home as part of the Harriet Tubman National Historical Park and her gravesite in the local Fort Hill Cemetery, but the destination had not gone further.

Kuhl and her team felt responsible for carrying into the future Harriet Tubman's legacy of lifting up community, and they identified her 200th birthday as the perfect occasion to emphasize her significance, to connect the people, businesses, and visitors of the area, and to build community pride.

Kuhl began with the foundation of her own organization. She knew that the Cayuga County Office of Tourism needed to be as strong as the marketing campaign they would use to reposition the community. They started by making sure diversity, equity, and inclusion were built into the tourism organization by revisiting their mission, vision, and values. Then they reviewed and updated internal documents, the board of directors' bylaws, their employee manuals, the plans of the committee and the board, and the make-up of the board itself.

They acknowledged that they needed more diversity on the Board of Directors and actively sought more diverse voices to add to the organization. Two new members were added, a Black woman from the local college, Dr. Rhoda Overstreet-Wilson, and the first Black legislator in their county, Brian Muldrow. In addition to these new board seats, the tourism office created a guiding coalition that eventually became the Equal Rights and Harriet Tubman Communications Committee. This committee was made up of community supporters, representatives from the historical sites that aligned with Tubman, and also community members who had an interest in helping to preserve her legacy, including her direct descendants. This committee was the sounding board for initiatives that would become part of the 200th birthday celebration and the repositioning of the community.

The foundation was established for this DEI-focused collaboration among Kuhl and her staff, the Cayuga County

Tourism Board of Directors, and the Communications Committee. The next step was to outline the initiatives that would be part of the community's repositioning and the 200th birthday campaign.

This initiative was more than a campaign; it was a holistic look at Harriet Tubman, the city of Auburn, the tourism assets that she touched, and local businesses and residents. Each aspect was thoughtfully considered and scrutinized through the lens of Tubman and DEI.

Tourism marketers like Cayuga County are storytellers. They help visitors understand the places they visit by shining a light on the whole community and what is unique there. The story that Cayuga County shared about Harriet Tubman went well beyond the assets specifically related to her. Instead, they revealed a broader narrative of her hometown and why she'd chosen to settle there. These stories took on many through lines including highlighting the streets where she walked, the stores she went to, the market where she sold her pigs, the family who sold her property, and all the parts of the community she had influenced.

It is not only the locations that make a place special, but also the people who live there, so Cayuga County decided to dig into who Harriet Tubman was outside of being a conductor on the Underground Railroad. More story threads were identified to share all the facets of who Tubman was while living in Auburn for fifty-four years. Working with partners, Cayuga County was able to uncover her many iden-tities—a Civil War military leader, a spy, a cook, a nurse, and a forager. These different aspects help paint a more detailed picture of who she was and how her legacy lives on through the community today.

When Kuhl and her partners started on this path, they wanted to highlight Black-owned businesses in the community as part of their efforts, even if those businesses were not tourism related. They found only a handful, and another opportunity was discovered. Through the repositioning of the community, they hoped to attract new businesses to the area that might align with Tubman's values, specifically Black-owned businesses. They began to work with the Cayuga County Economic Development Agency and the Downtown Business Improvement District to discuss how they could use their new position to reach and incentivize businesses to locate there.

The collaborative program continued to expand to include outreach to the residents of the community. Many locals did not know that they lived in Harriet Tubman's hometown or the pivotal role the community had played in the equal rights movement. They conducted interviews with key community members and residents to find out why they were proud to live in Tubman's chosen hometown. Then they created yard signs and window stickers for residents and businesses to display that read: AUBURN, NY: Proud to Live in Harriet Tubman's Chosen Hometown. They worked with local leaders, businesses, and key community members to help get the message out.

Another important component of this initiative was to provide DEI training to businesses and front-line staff in the community. Getting the welcome right and being authentic were critical to this work, and visitors would see right through it if the messaging did not match the experience. The Cayuga County Office of Tourism Board of Directors designated funds to conduct training for local businesses and their staffs. This included assisting with the development of DEI statements to add to tourism business websites and helping the community understand how to live up to them.

Kuhl and her community continue to work collaboratively to incorporate DEI into everything they do, to attract new audiences, and to build community pride. Harriet Tubman's 200th birthday celebration was a catalyst to get these initiatives started, and even though the birthday has passed, these programs live on as part of her legacy.

You can hear the whole story on episode 295 of *Destination on the Left* at:

> To listen to the interview, visit:
> https://nicolemahoney.com/stronger-together-resources

Improving Inclusion with Collaboration: Mesa, AZ

Diversity, Equity, and Inclusion (DEI) is coming to the forefront of everyone's mind in the travel and tourism industry. In my interview with Marc Garcia from Visit Mesa, he shared his personal passion for making his community a fun place to visit for all travelers by becoming the first autism-certified city in the United States.

Garcia had experience with multicultural initiatives throughout his career, from working for the Phoenix Multicultural Arts Foundation to running a multicultural affairs department focused on attracting ethnic meetings and conventions to his community. Even with that experience, the idea to focus on autism in Mesa came from his youngest son who was diagnosed with severe autism at fourteen months of age. Garcia explained his family's journey to figure out how to care for their son, what his needs were, and where to obtain the services he required. Living their lives included summer-time family vacations and a tradition of travelling to Southern California and spending a lazy week at the beach. One summer, they decided to immerse themselves in the city to try different restaurants and visit museums and attractions. They split their vacation time equally between the beach and the city, but Garcia reported that the family had a really bad week as his son had meltdown after meltdown. He described the awkward stares and muffled whispers that the family would get when his son acted up, most notably from hospi-tality professionals in hotels, restaurants, and attractions. That was when Garcia decided that he wanted to do something to make it easier for families of people with autism to travel and enjoy a vacation together.

Visit Mesa was in the middle of a three-year strategic plan, and Garcia presented the idea of becoming autism-friendly to his Board of Directors. He had done some research and had discovered that ten years ago, one in 100 kids was diagnosed with autism; by 2018, it's closer to one in fifty-eight and now in 2022, it's one in forty-four. Garcia knew this was a loyal customer base and a growing market which helped him make the business case for his big idea. Not only

was it the right thing to do, it was also a good business decision if they could get out in front of the market. The Board
of Directors and the staff at Visit Mesa bought into the idea,
and in the fall of 2018, they started to build a collaboration
to make Mesa the first autism-certified city in the country.

Since Garcia's son was getting resources from local
organizations, he started working through his network to find
someone to provide education to the hospitality industry,
hoping to find a certification program. He couldn't find any
locally, so he searched nationally and came across the International Board of Credentialing and Continuing Education
Standards based in Jacksonville, Florida. The organization
had autism-certified school boards, public safety groups, and
healthcare and educational professionals, and they had begun
certifying hotels and attractions scattered across the
country—but never an entire city. Garcia had several conversations with their Board of Directors, and together, they deter-
mined that if Mesa could get fifty-eight of their hospitality
businesses and 80 percent of their front-line staff to go
through this educational program, they could achieve certification as an autism-certified travel destination. The first
focus was the destination and not the whole city.

The Visit Mesa staff went through the program in
February 2019 and rolled out a community-wide launch that
April. They partnered with five other organizations including
the Chamber of Commerce, the City Parks Department, and
three of their largest hotels. They engaged the Mayor of Mesa
and had him on camera carrying the message of why the
initiative was important. Garcia described the domino effect

that happened after launch as "unbelievable," with business after business signing on to be part of the certification program. With the outreach through the mayor's office and the Chamber of Commerce, many businesses outside of the hospitality industry saw the certification program as a workforce recruitment tool and started to sign on, including Boeing, local auto shops, and a major utility company, and the program kept growing.

By the late summer of 2019, Mesa had exceeded the requirement of fifty-eight businesses, and they had trained almost 5,000 people. With that success, they announced in November of 2019 that Mesa was the first autism-certified city in the country. They received a lot of great press stories with coverage from the *LA Times*, *The New York Times*, BBC, and other top-tier outlets. They have now booked several meetings and conferences because of the designation which Garcia says brought them strong ROI right from the start.

Garcia credits the ongoing effort beyond the certification as critical to this collaboration's success. For example, on April 2, 2022, World Autism Awareness Day and the start of National Autism Awareness Month, they partnered with two microbreweries for a special beer release, Spectrum Double IPA. This partnership supports the autism-certified city while promoting Mesa's burgeoning beer scene. A portion of the proceeds from beer sales go to support the recently formed Mesa Regional Foundation for Accessibility, Diversity, and Inclusion. This foundation was established to work on programs that further the cause with the first pilot program focused on introducing high school students from Title I schools to career opportunities in the hospitality industry. They are also developing a pilot program for sixth through twelfth graders who have an affinity for gaming, which many kids on the spectrum do. This program is in partnership with Arizona State University—the college has a brand-new campus opening in downtown Mesa that will offer majors in artificial intelligence, augmented reality, virtual reality, gaming, and coding.

Garcia built a collaboration that has far-reaching impacts. Not only is he making a difference in his community, he is also making life easier for families of people with autism.

You can hear the whole story on episode 275 of *Destination on the Left*.

To listen to the interview, visit:
https://nicolemahoney.com/stronger-together-resources

CHAPTER 10

Cathedral Thinking

Cathedral Thinking is about having a vision that has such far-reaching impact that when you start to work toward the vision, you do so with the knowledge that you will not be around to see it completed. The concept goes back to Medieval times when an architect, stonemason, and artisan began construction on the large buildings that would become places of worship, community gathering spaces, and safe havens. These visionaries would begin their work knowing that it would not be completed in their lifetime, maybe not even their children's lifetime, and in some cases it would be three generations before the project was complete. These were world-changing collaborations that created a future bigger and brighter than any one person could have done on their own. Much of what we are doing today is setting in motion projects and ideas that will have far-reaching impact. Imagine what is possible when you think beyond the boundaries of one lifetime.

Cathedral Thinking in Action

Author and speaker, Rick Antonson, says that Cathedral Thinking is synonymous with long-term planning, creating a shared vision, and working collaboratively. Cathedral Thinking is a key ingredient for creating a world-changing collaboration, and applying this type of long-term thinking to the 3-C Framework for Collaboration will exponentially increase your opportunity for success.

In a podcast interview with Antonson, he expanded on the concept. If in the 15th century, you were an architect in your community, and your city asked you to design a new cathedral, you would begin that work knowing that you would not live to see that project completed. It may be a grandchild or the grandchild of a neighbor who did the final renderings. Likewise, if you were a stonemason, putting in place the cornerstone or the foundation blocks, you would not be around when the spire was completed. You would be putting in place a foundation that someone else in the craft could build upon. In building a cathedral, it was about doing something every day that contributed toward the total edifice, toward the long-term vision.

Cathedral Thinking is the only way to keep the living generation tethered to the future. It's about doing things today that are very important for beneficiaries who may not be born yet. It helps us in a simple way to conceive of the importance of long-term thinking, of being involved in unfinished work. Seeing that what we do today has to have a way to be built upon, not just by a colleague in contemporary times, but by a son or daughter or a future colleague who may join your firm or organization or community long after you yourself have left it. Cathedral Thinking is keeping in mind that the details, the importance, and the integrity with which we approach today's work need to be able to be applicable for others who will bring new tools, apply the fresh skills of a new generation, and continue the good work.

Practicing this type of thinking starts with awareness of the moment. What was isn't, and what is won't be. We are transitory in the nature of the work we do. It is our moment to do the best we can and to set up our successors for their own elements of success. By thinking in that way, we bring a different element of sincerity to the current workload because we know it is not about us. It's about what we are doing. It's about the task at hand and being able to enable others to do their jobs better. It could be a colleague. It could be someone in your community. It could be people within a task force that has seemingly short-term timelines. But when done, it has to have accomplished something that is the start of whatever somebody else does next. It's about how this moment shapes the future.

Having that self-awareness is as important now as it was in the 1400s, when they were literally laying building blocks for the future. In life, you are constantly laying a foundation and building upon it. And you never really finish, even if you are able to check it off your to-do list.

Some of our systems are set up to impede this type of thinking. Elected officials at all levels are voted into office with a specific mandate making it difficult for them to think or act beyond their tenure. Elected officials often have a self-imposed horizon which happens to be the next election. Whether it's six months or two years away, that's how far ahead they look. They are fixated on the near-term and are not able look more than thirty or forty years down the road. To create world-changing collaborations, we need our elected officials to think beyond their mandate and act beyond their tenure.

For example, the community may need a convention center expansion that could take ten years to complete. If the city council term is up in another year and the project will not activate for four, the project needs a champion with great foresight so decisions can be made today to set the project in motion. One way to work within this system is to get elected officials to embrace organizations like the Destination Marketing Organization and other entities with the vision of where the city or region is going to be in ten to thirty years. When we embrace this approach, long-lasting collaborations can take place more effectively.

Cathedral Thinking and the long term are both intergenerational, happening for decades down the road. It's like bidding for the Olympics, then twenty years later, the games are finally in your community. The 2010 Winter Olympics were scheduled for Vancouver, Canada, but the city needed to make infrastructure investments to prepare for them. There was a proposal to develop rapid transit that would connect the airport, the community of Richmond, and downtown Vancouver. It was necessary for hosting the Olympics, but elected officials turned it down twice. The Destination Marketing Organization was very involved in lobbying and forming a consortium of a hundred different entities that pushed for a third vote, which was ultimately successful. The rapid transit opened in time for the Olympics, and in the early months of operation, it far exceeded ridership forecasts and was viewed as a glowing success.

Cathedral Thinking has been extremely good for the environment, allowing people to put plans in motion to mitigate the long-term impacts of climate change. Cathedral Thinkers recognize the science and understand the impact it will have decades down the road. It doesn't have to be something big like the Olympics, but every day, everyone has to be doing something that is building—not just repairing or making wishes—but taking actual short-term actions that build toward the future. Most of us internationally are making small decisions today with tenacious plans to follow-through with a long-term view in mind for our communities, businesses, and personal lives.

Ellsworth M. Statler and Kemmons Wilson were two historical Cathedral Thinkers who helped shape the travel industry. Statler was a hotel developer who coined the phrase "the customer is always right." He created the first hotel that catered to the middle class, opening the Statler Hotel in Buffalo, New York, in 1907. This hotel set standards for comfort and convenience that changed the industry. In 1952, Wilson created a new business model for roadside hotels. The hotels offered perks that many customers take for granted today—air-conditioned rooms, free parking, free ice, and rates by the room instead of by the person. That business model created the first Holiday Inn and changed the hospitality industry for generations.

> To listen to Rick Antonson's interview visit:
> https://nicolemahoney.com/stronger-together-resources

Destination Cleveland

In a podcast interview with David Gilbert, CEO of Destination Cleveland, he shares his perspective on how his organization is re-thinking the visitor for the long-term benefit of the community. Destination Cleveland is a convention and visitors bureau funded largely by an occupancy tax that the hotels collect. Many cities formed these types of organizations decades ago on the same funding model, which focuses the organization on short-term goals. These goals are measured by room nights, number of visitors, dollars spent, jobs created, and tax revenue generated, but these are all short-term. David's organization began to realize that not every visitor is created equal, and that there was an unrealized opportunity in the much longer term.

By thinking of Cleveland as a branded product and visitors as Cleveland's customers, the organization began to think not only about the dollars that customers were spending, but also about the influence those customers had on changing perceptions about the community. Research had shown that someone who has visited a place is more likely to become a resident of that place compared to someone who has never been there before, like a first date, and Destination Cleveland wanted to figure out how to convert some of those first dates into marriages. With millions of visitors coming to Cleveland each year for leisure, business meetings, and conventions, the community had a larger opportunity to attract new talent and investment depending on whether they could convert a percentage of those visitors into residents.

As part of a talent attraction strategy, Destination Cleveland helped change perceptions of the community. They pulled together a collaborative partnership that includes a cross-section of what the city offers and has emphasized these insights through marketing, destination branding, and economic development. Today, they are still focused on using the Cleveland brand beyond filling the top of the funnel with visitors; they are carrying the message all the way to the bottom of the funnel and converting them into residents, students, and business investors. By taking a larger view of the organization, the visitor, and their ability to impact the community in lasting ways, Destination Cleveland is applying Cathedral Thinking to creating a better tomorrow for future generations.

To listen to the interview with David Gilbert visit:
https://nicolemahoney.com/stronger-together-resources

North Coast Harbor

North Coast Harbor, located on the shore of Lake Erie in Cleveland, is another example of cathedral thinking in action. Since the late 1800s, the City of Cleveland recognized the importance of its shoreline, with many developments coming and going over the years, but in 1985, North Coast Harbor, Inc. was created to plan and manage the development of 176 acres of lakefront properties. The district today is home to world-class venues, including the Rock and Roll Hall of Fame and Museum, the Great Lakes Science Center, and FirstEnergy Stadium, home of the Cleveland Browns. These unique places sit alongside public spaces, residential apartments, retail shops, restaurants, and activity providers.

In a podcast interview with Dr. Kirsten Ellenbogen, President of Great Lakes Science Center in Cleveland and one of the primary stakeholders in North Coast Harbor, Dr. Ellenbogen described the positive energy that comes from being part of a group of stakeholders who consider things from a generational perspective. As new developments are planned and needs change, the collective is working together with a common vision to create the next iteration of the North Coast Shore that will enhance accessibility and elevate visitor experiences.

The Great Lakes Science Center also collaborates with

the NASA Glen Research Center, which through cooperation was designated the visitor center for their Ohio-based location. As one of only eleven NASA Visitor Centers designated by Congress, the Great Lakes Science Center understands the importance of this collaboration and the impacts this identity makes on city tourism. The collaborative team that oversees and guides the visitor center includes policy makers, scientists, community members, board members, and staff. The role of the visitor center is to get the public excited about the research that NASA scientists and engineers are doing. This type of program helps draw national and international audiences to the museum.

To hear to Dr. Kirsten Ellenbogen story, visit: https://nicolemahoney.com/stronger-together-resources

Creation Through Collaboration

Often, what appears to be an overnight success is actually the result of long-term planning done behind the scenes long before the finished product is unveiled.

Successful collaborations have a shared vision for the future, as was the case when Dr. Annette Rummel, CEO of the Great Lakes Bay Regional Convention and Visitors Bureau (CVB), led the effort to execute an idea years in the making—since 1986, to be precise—combining three county CVB organizations into one regional CVB. This collaboration would reduce overhead expenses for each county's CVB and generate additional revenue for marketing and advertising to encourage travel to the area and tourism throughout.

The opportunity to bring this idea to fruition presented itself in 2009, when Rummel was serving as CEO of the Saginaw County Convention and Visitors Bureau. In response to the year's economic downturn, she was asked to take over management of Midland and Bay counties' convention and visitors bureaus. Rummel initially hesitated, however, based on the difficulty of getting a piece of state legislation passed that would allow their assessments to be adjusted during a time of political tension. So Rummel made a deal with the board of Saginaw County's CVB: if both Midland and Bay County could agree on this plan, they'd move forward. And to her surprise, they did—unanimously. The Bay County Board of Commissioners would also later approve this merger.

Collaborative Funding

Rummel knew that she would need the support of State lawmakers in order to establish the regional CVB. With the commitments of all three counties, she set her sights on Lansing and getting the legislation required to establish the Great Lakes Regional Convention and Visitors Bureau. She started with a statewide caucus that included every elected official who represented any part of the three-county region. From local to state and federal officials, she invited everyone to participate. Rummel held monthly meetings to keep the caucus apprised of their progress and focused on the goal of creating a regional CVB that would be responsible for marketing while maintaining tourism-related economic development projects focused on the county level.

With all three counties committed to the merger and the common goal of bringing more tourism to the area, there was the matter of funding to consider—specifically, the disparity between the three counties' budgets, Bay County with $156,000, Midland County with $275,000 and Saginaw County with $1 million. How could they bring these entities together with such vast differences in investment revenue? The solution was to level the playing field by collecting 5 percent room tax assessments in each county, as well as offering up to a $750 tax credit each quarter with proof of paid chamber membership dues or advertising receipts. In addition to leveling the playing field on the revenue side, each county would realize significant savings on expenses, leading to more money to invest in economic development projects in marketing and tourism.

To achieve the newly formed CVBs' goal of moving marketing up to the regional level while still maintaining the identity for each of the county CVBs, each county CVB would continue to receive their funds directly. Their local boards then moved 75 percent of their funds directly to the regional CVB for marketing and advertising. This meant counties retained 25 percent, more than what was needed for overhead, allowing each one to establish a tourism economic development budget.

Collaboration is good for business, and the Go Great Lakes Bay Regional CVB proves it. Over the period from 2009 through 2018, each county in the region increased collections; Bay County went from $156,000 to $830,000, Midland County went from $275,000 to $1,100,000 and Saginaw went from $1,000,000 to $1,900,000. Each county has more money for marketing and for tourism economic development projects.

Here's a quick break-down of the results of Rummel's CVB collaboration:

- There was a 370 percent increase in marketing efforts across the board.

- The collaboration reduced overhead expenses across the board by 54 percent.

- The Saginaw Township Soccer Complex was expanded from sixteen contiguous fields to twenty-one.

- Two properties in disrepair were removed, paving the way for Saginaw County to establish the Huntington Event Park, a soundstage and outdoor venue for art exhibits and outdoor concerts.

- The regional CVB's office was constructed in a $16 million facility in Midland County, with one of the condominiums purchased outright.

Through the process, the regional CVB also became certified through the Destination Marketing Accreditation Program (DMAP). The merger also proved to be an eye-opening lesson in operational efficiency, highlighting opportunities for collaboration among economic development offices, chamber of commerce operations, and destination marketing and management efforts, as well as eliminating duplicate tasks.

Rummel's foresight and problem-solving strategies are incredible examples of how collaboration combined with Cathedral Thinking can yield profitable results for the present and for generations to come.

To learn more about the formation of the Go Great Lakes Bay Regional CVB, listen to my interview with Annette Rummel.

Hear Annette Rummel's story here:
https://nicolemahoney.com/stronger-together-resources

CHAPTER 11

Collaborating Through Uncertainty

Most of us remember where we were on 9/11 and how the world changed that day. The economy suffered after 9/11, and we rebuilt stronger than before. We felt the pain from the 2008 economic downturn and the impact it had on our industry, yet we rebounded to record high numbers. Then the COVID-19 pandemic caused the world's borders to close in the name of social distancing and flattening the curve. We were immediately affected by lockdowns and the reliance of the world economy on the ability of people and goods to continuously flow across the continents. Suddenly, we were all in this together, and our robust growing economy came to a screeching halt.

Early in the pandemic, I found a video of Simon Sinek talking to his team over Zoom after the start of the lockdown in the US. He was explaining to his team that he just had an epiphany of sorts. It was a pep talk that was brilliant, raw, and real. He told his team, "These are not unprecedented times. There are many cases where change or something unexpected has put many companies out of business and made other companies come out stronger and reinvent themselves." He then went on to explain that the difference between closure and reinvention is the difference between a finite mindset and an infinite one. For me, it's the choice between operating out of scarcity and fear or growth and abundance.

Many examples from our past prove there is precedent for crises like the 2020 pandemic. For example, the sharing economy was born as a new game plan after the 2008 global financial crisis to stimulate the economy by creating new business models. Companies like Uber, Lyft, Airbnb, and WeWork are now commonplace, and these businesses have changed our society.

We are at our creative best when faced with a challenge or period of adversity. As the saying goes, never let a crisis go to waste. Companies who keep a forward-thinking mindset can re-imagine how the world does business. As Sinek says, "To live our lives with an infinite mindset, means that we are driven to advance a cause bigger than ourselves." Mindset plays a big role in how we respond to a crisis. The

COVID-19 pandemic was six crises in one, deeply impacting public health, business, the economy, the dissemination of information, government oversight, and the very fabric of our society. It's no wonder people felt an array of emotions. Those emotions are okay, but as leaders—of organizations, communities, and families—it is how we choose to respond that makes a real impact.

If we learned only one thing from the global pandemic, it's that we are all in this together—that our world is inter-connected, and we must work as a team to build a future that benefits us all. The new normal will rely on collaborations more than ever before. In fact, there is one major world-changing collaboration that helps illustrate how having the right mindset and finding the right partners can lead to a huge impact. It is the story of mRNA technology and the develop-ment of the COVID-19 vaccine.

Dr. Katalin Kariko is a Hungarian biochemist who played a central role in the development of the vaccines that helped slow the pandemic and bring it to an end. Dr. Kariko grew up in Hungary and studied biology in college and graduate school. While earning her doctorate, she learned about a recently discovered molecule called messenger RNA, which serves as a liaison between DNA and cells within the body. The discovery of mRNA fascinated Kariko, and she saw the potential for changing the message to control the way the cells behaved, helping people with chronic illnesses.

This discovery happened in the 1970s, and many scien-tists thought it was impossible to change the message because they didn't know how to make it. But Kariko had an infinite mindset; she could see the possibilities, and she was committed to pushing the discovery further. Then, the Hungarian lab where she was working on her PhD ran out of money.

That did not stop her from pursuing her research, however, and eventually Kariko moved to the US, where she landed a job at the University of Pennsylvania. While working as a research assistant, she set up several experiments to make a cell produce something it normally didn't. She made a breakthrough in her research and proved that the message in mRNA could be changed after all. Then, the scientist she was working with left the university, leaving Kariko again without a lab.

Kariko's infinite mindset kept her moving forward, and she sought grants to continue her research. By that time, it was the early 1990s, and none of her grant proposals were funded. In one case, a grant fund was planning to award grants to six applicants. Seven researchers submitted applications, and the one not funded was hers. Kariko's persistence was exceptional against the norms of academic research work conditions, so she continued to pursue her vision and seek other opportunities to continue her work.

In 1997, she met Drew Weissman, professor of immunology at the University of Pennsylvania who was working on a vaccine and took interest in the mRNA research that Kariko was pursuing. Dr. Weissman invited her to join his lab, and the two of them began working side-by-side to try to make mRNA manipulate the cells within a live organism. The two scientists made progress on the research and began publishing articles about the new technology in 2005.

After a lecture in 2013, Kariko met the founder of a small tech start-up called BioNTech. He was interested in mRNA technology, understood Kariko's vision, and offered her a job on the spot. Shortly after that, Pfizer and BioNTech partnered with the idea to collaborate on an mRNA vaccine, and both companies signed an agreement in 2018 to prepare the technology to fight influenza. When COVID-19 hit, BioNTech realized they were in a unique position because they already knew from working on the flu vaccine how to manipulate mRNA for medical applications. Production was already well-advanced and ready for human trials.

It was clear to Dr. Kariko and Dr. Weissman that the concept they had been pursuing for decades could do the work of training the body to fight the coronavirus. A normal vaccine would take forever to produce, but with their unique position, all they had to do was figure out what protein the virus used to infect cells. Instead of an influenza-specific sequence, they inserted the SARS-CoV-2 sequence into the messenger. In 2020, the technology created by Kariko and Weissman was expedited to fight COVID-19, and was mass-produced jointly by Pfizer and BioNTech.

Hear more about Katalin's story:

> To listen to the interview, visit:
> https://nicolemahoney.com/stronger-together-resources

Collaboration, In Conclusion

Kariko's story illustrates the power of combining a forward-thinking mindset with collaboration. As Zig Ziglar said, "Sometimes adversity is what you need to face in order to become successful." Collaboration is at the heart of every solution to our biggest and most complex problems. When you open yourself up to the power of partnership and the possibilities collaboration can bring, the results truly are exponential. There were countless examples throughout this book that prove we are stronger together.

While our research showed that there are many obstacles and challenges to collaboration, the benefits of working together far outweigh the challenges. The strategies and tools outlined in this book will help you create more streamlined approaches to working with other organizations to accomplish your goals. Collaboration, even between competing businesses, makes good business sense and leads to better outcomes for all parties involved. I hope the stories, framework, tools, and creative approaches to collaboration in this book have inspired you to think bigger, find your biggest opportunity, and figure out how to work together to achieve success.

Cathedral Thinking will magnify your success and increase the impacts you can make in your corner of the world. You are one of the leaders, visionaries, and great thinkers that will help define your industry for the next generation. What world-changing collaborations will you pursue?

ACKNOWLEDGMENTS

Writing a book is a big endeavor and can seem unattainable without the right support system to help you make it happen. In making my list for this section of the book, I put down on paper what I already knew: I am blessed to have a huge circle of support around me. This circle has carried me through my life, opened my eyes to new possibilities, and taught me that I can accomplish anything I set my mind to.

First, my husband, John Mahoney, who has loved me for over 30 years. Without you I would not have been able to pursue the things I am most passionate about. Your encouragement and willingness to take care of the home front while I focus on my work made this book possible. Thank you for your never-ending commitment and dedication. I love you, infinity!

To my four daughters Morgan, Maeve, Margaux, and Marley, you bring purpose to my life; without you I would not be as passionate about creating a better future. You are the future, and I am thankful that I am your mom.

My mother, Kristine Niven, thank you for always being willing to lend a listening ear, for encouraging me to pursue my dreams, and for loving me unconditionally.

To my father, Jim Wemett, you have always been my rock, the one I lean on when I need help, the one I go to for practical advice, and the one who has always believed that I can do anything.

My sister, Jaime Saunders, thank you for being a great

lil' sis, you have always encouraged me, and you are my biggest cheerleader. Thank you for teaching me how to embrace the world, what true caring for others looks like, and how to make service to others a priority. You are an inspiration to me.

To my Aunt Sandy & Uncle Carmen Pagano, thank you for being part of my A-team, always willing to jump in and help, listening to my speech rehearsals and for cheering me on.

I was blessed to have many mentors early in my career who made an impact on me and helped me find my true passion. Thank you to Jim LeBeau for taking a chance on hiring me in 1994 and showing me how to be a true community ambassador; your passion for the Rochester region and the impact you made throughout your career inspired me to pursue my interests in search of greater purpose.

I am forever grateful to Greg Marshall who has been a mentor and cheerleader for nearly 30 years. Thank you for teaching me how to be a true steward of a destination, what support for the local business community looks like, and how passion can turn into a rewarding career with lifelong friendships.

To Seran & John Wilkie, I am grateful for the day that you walked into my office which led to decades of friendship, compassion, and coaching. The lessons that I learned from one-on-one coaching with Seran helped shape me into the person I am today. Thank you for taking me under your wing and teaching me how to live a happier, less stressful life even with the ups and downs that come with the journey.

Finding your tribe is a wonderful thing, when you meet people who share similar interests, values, and passion you feel like you are home. I am blessed to have found many tribes throughout my life journey.

I am grateful to Bobbie Goheen of Synthesis Management Group for her guidance, coaching, and friendship. She has created a community of leaders who are striving to connect their minds and their hearts to become better leaders, friends, family members, and better humans in general. I am forever thankful that I have my network of heart leadership women, Staci Henning, Nicole Savage, Leslie Connolly, Jill Peterson, Andrea Fitzgerald, who have encouraged me to pursue this book and all my passions.

Having friends you can count on, who are always willing to lend an ear or a helping hand or who you can just hang out with enjoying a glass of wine and some cards is a blessing. I am grateful to my BFFs Rhonda Carges, Michelle Meyer, Kate Hagberg, and Cherie Malloy who have been through the good and bad times together and always cheer me on as I pursue my life's work.

My work team is my tribe, and I am grateful that we have found each other in pursuit of a common vision and in service to the travel, tourism, and hospitality industry. Without my team, this book would not be possible, from helping me create content around our views of collaboration, to assisting with my podcast Destination on the Left, to taking care of our clients while I pursue my dreams of becoming a speaker and an author. I am forever grateful to the BTI team Rhonda Carges, Lisa Doerner, Mary Eggert. Brittany Lynn, Sarah

Martin, Adena Miller, Colleen Onuffer, and Camille Zess.

Thanks to Drew McClellan and the Agency Management Institute family. I am grateful to this group for providing me with the best practices, tools, and inspiration to grow my company into a purpose-driven organization with a specific niche and audience. I am thankful for the many people I have met through my AMI Momentum Peer Network and the extended AMI community. Without Drew and AMI, I would not have found my focus and this book would not have come to pass. Thank you for your service in helping small business owners like me find our north star.

To Susan Baier and Audience Audit, thank you for your help with the collaboration research that validated my thinking in this space and provided me with new data and information to share with the world.

Stephen Woessner, Erik Jansen, and the Predictive ROI team, I am grateful to have you as a strategic partner in all of the work that I do. Your help with the launch and production of my podcast Destination on the Left is the foundation for what this book is built on. Your mentorship and guidance on everything from podcasting to writing a book have made my journey a lot easier and more enjoyable.

To the Heroic Public Speaking community and Michael and Amy Port, thank you for helping me find my big idea and for giving me the courage to share it with the world. And thank you to my HPS Lab group for your mentorship, encouragement, and camaraderie. Since 2021, I have spent Tuesdays and Thursdays on zoom with Jennifer Fondrevay, Kris Kelso, Paula White, Julie Ellis, Carol Stizza, Pam Harper, and Sharon Preszler. You are an inspirational group, and I am blessed to have you in my life.

Thank you to the guests of my podcast Destination on the Left. Your willingness to share your experiences and ideas have helped shape this book.

A heartfelt thanks to Bookpress Publishing and my book coach and mentor, Tony Paustian. Without your guidance and assistance this book would still be an idea in my head. Thank you for your feedback, nudging, and encouragement.